2007-Eleven

2007-Eleven

AND OTHER AMERICAN COMEDIES

Frank Cammuso and Hart Seely

VILLARD

NEW YORK

Library of Congress Cataloging-in-Publication Data
Cammuso, Frank
2007-eleven : and other American comedies / Frank Cammuso
and Hart Seely.—1st ed.
p.   cm.
ISBN 0-375-50412-5
1. American wit and humor.   I. Title: Two thousand seven-eleven.
II. Seely, Hart.   III. Title.
PN6162.S355 2000
818′.602—dc21   99-044112

Villard Books website address: www.villard.com

Printed in the United States of America on acid-free paper

2   4   6   8   9   7   5   3

First Edition

Book designed by Fritz Metsch

Some of the essays in this work have previously appeared in *National
Lampoon, The New Republic, The New York Times, The New York Times
Magazine, The New Yorker, Slate,* and *Spy Magazine.*

Grateful acknowledgment is made to the Syracuse Newspapers for
permission to reprint "Witch v. Dorothy," which appeared as an editorial
in the June 4, 1999, issue of *The Post-Standard.* The Herald Co. © 1999
The Post-Standard. All rights reserved. Reprinted with permission.

For Mom and Dad

—— F R A N K

For Whitcraft

—— S E E L Y

Contents

Contents

2007-Eleven

The Xmas Files

Elm Street

Bethlehem, Pa.

11:51 P.M. December 24

We're too late! It's already been here.

Mulder, I hope you know what you're doing.

Look, Scully—just like the other homes: Douglas fir, truncated, mounted, transformed into a shrine . . . halls decked with boughs of holly . . . stockings hung by the chimney, with care.

You really think someone's been here?

Someone . . . or something.

Mulder, over here—it's a fruitcake . . .

Don't touch it! Those things can be lethal!

It's OK. There's a note attached: "Gonna find out who's naughty and nice."

It's judging them, Scully. It's making a list.

Who? What are you talking about?

Ancient mythology tells of an obese humanoid

entity who could travel at great speed in a craft powered by antlered servants. Once each year, near the winter solstice, this creature is said to descend from the heavens to reward its followers and punish disbelievers with jagged chunks of anthracite.

But that's legend, Mulder—a story told by parents to frighten children. Surely you don't believe it?

Something was here tonight, Scully. Check out the bite marks on this gingerbread man. Whatever tore through this plate of cookies was massive—and in a hurry.

It left crumbs everywhere. And look, Mulder, this milk glass has been completely drained.

It gorged itself, Scully. It fed without remorse.

But why would they leave it milk and cookies?

Appeasement. Tonight is the Eve, and nothing can stop its wilding.

But if this thing does exist, how did it get in? The doors and windows were locked. There's no sign of forced entry.

Unless I miss my guess, it came through the fireplace.

Wait a minute, Mulder. If you're saying some huge creature landed on the roof and came down this chimney, you're crazy. The flue is barely six inches wide. Nothing could get down there.

But what if it could alter its shape, move in all directions at once?

You mean, like a bowl full of jelly?

Exactly. Scully, I've never told anyone this, but when I was a child, my home was visited. I saw the creature. It had long white shanks of fur surrounding its ruddy, misshapen head. Its bloated torso was red and white. I'll never forget the horror. I turned away, and when I looked back, it had somehow taken on the facial features of my father.

Impossible.

I know what I saw. And that night, it read my mind. It brought me a Mr. Potato Head, Scully. *It knew that I wanted a Mr. Potato Head!*

I'm sorry, Mulder, but you're asking me to disregard the laws of physics. You want me to believe in some supernatural being who soars across the skies and brings gifts to good little girls and boys. Listen to what you're saying. Do you understand the repercussions? If this gets out, they'll close the X files.

Scully, listen to me: It knows when you're sleeping. It knows when you're awake.

But we have no proof.

Last year on this exact date, SETI radio telescopes detected bogeys in the airspaces over twenty-seven states. The White House ordered a Condition Red.

But that was a meteor shower.

Officially. Two days ago, eight prized Scandinavian reindeer vanished from the National Zoo in Washington, D.C. Nobody—not even the zookeeper—was told about it. The government doesn't want people to know about Project Kringle. They fear that if this thing is proved to exist, the public will stop spending half its annual income in a holiday shopping frenzy. Retail markets will collapse. Scully, they cannot let the world believe this creature lives. There's too much at stake. They'll do whatever it takes to ensure another silent night.

Mulder, I—

Sh-h-h. Do you hear what I hear?

On the roof. It sounds like . . . a clatter.

The truth is up there. Let's see what's the matter.

Witch v. Dorothy

||||||||||||||||||||||||||||||||||||||||||||||||||||||||||||||||||||||||||||||||||||||||||||||||||||||||||

IN U.S. DISTRICT COURT, DISTRICT OF KANSAS

WICKED WITCH OF WEST, a supernatural being and MBA (Mistress of Black Arts) licensed to operate in the merry land of Oz.

Plaintiff.

-v-

DOROTHY G., a minor; EM and HENRY G., guardians; GLINDA, a self-proclaimed "good witch"; OZ, a wonderful wizard if ever a wiz there was; LOYAL ORDER OF THE LOLLIPOP GUILD, INC., a fraternal organization; EMERALD CITY INDUSTRIAL DEVELOPMENT AUTHORITY, et al.

Defendants.

I. INTRODUCTION AND SUMMARY

Plaintiff seeks monetary and damage relief, resulting from denial of Civil Rights, as described under the United States Constitution, through broad-based conspiracy of high-ranking officials; including unlawful discrimination based on religious practice and crossing a rainbow with intent to commit a felony.

II. UNDISPUTED FACTS

1. OIQn or about June 5, 1939, following a dispute over local leash laws, Defendant DOROTHY G. ran away from home.

2. Upon information and belief, DOROTHY G. secured and piloted a thirty-four-ton farmhouse through a cyclone, relocating said dwelling onto property not zoned for residential use. Furthermore, said dwelling violated numerous codes requiring equal access for Munchkin Americans.

3. Upon learning of fatal injuries to Plaintiff's sister, Wicked Witch of East, DOROTHY G. told bystanders without remorse that "the house began

to pitch, the kitchen took a slitch, and landed . . . in the middle of a ditch," crushing to death said witch.

4. After learning that victim was "not only merely dead [but] really most sincerely dead," DOROTHY G. removed evidence in the form of the deceased's bejeweled footwear, treasured family heirlooms. Defendant then fled crime scene, wearing said evidence, claiming immunity from prosecution because she was not "in Kansas anymore."

5. Through coercion and deceit, DOROTHY G. recruited as agent subordinate a mental incompetent (henceforth known as SCARECROW), who was employed in the agricultural industry as a security guard, despite displaying on repeated standardized tests an IQ of zero.

6. Through coercion and fraud, DOROTHY G. recruited a robot (henceforth known as TINMAN), originally designed for lumber production, by offering said agent a surgical chest enhancement.

7. Through coercion and intimidation, DOROTHY G. recruited an endangered species (henceforth known as LION), known to exhibit psychotic ten-

dencies in a stated desire to make "the chipmunks genuflect to me," by offering said predator "courage."

8. Blood tests later revealed in DOROTHY G. and LION excessive concentrations of a poppy-based sedative, a controlled substance under Class C federal drug-law statutes. Also, both later admitted receiving from GLINDA a stimulant known by the street name "snow."

9. Upon arriving in Emerald City, DOROTHY G. and said agents entered into a verbal contract with OZ to serve as mercenaries in a mission to steal Plaintiff's broomstick, her lone means of transportation and a key to her livelihood in the field of commercial skywriting.

10. During assault inside Plaintiff's castle, DOROTHY G. threw an unknown liquid solvent upon Plaintiff, causing an immediate and acute allergic reaction.

11. Plaintiff melted.

12. Upon return to Emerald City, DOROTHY G. and OZ defrauded said agents:

a) Instead of increased mental capacity, SCARE-CROW received an associate's degree from Emerald City Community College.

b) Instead of an internal organ from a compatible donor, TINMAN received a clock.

c) Instead of "courage," LION received a "Land of Oz" medallion from the Franklin Mint, valued at $6.99.

III. CLAIM

1. DOROTHY G.'s actions caused Plaintiff physical, emotional, and financial distress, including loss of income, castle, and surrounding real estate, and thirty-five trained flying monkeys, valued at $20,000 per animal; also loss through waste of 144 crates of Purina Flying Monkey Chow.

2. Due to injuries sustained during meltdown, Plaintiff suffers chronic back pain and requires twenty-four-hour assisted mopping.

3. Plaintiff seeks compensation in form of $20 million, representing the assets of EM and HENRY G.'s shopping-mall outlets, "Lions and Tigers 'n' Things"; all Oz-copyrighted merchandise; and Toto, too.

Martha Stewart's Last Supper

You are cordially invited to a
Going-Away Dinner
for a truly Special Guest.
Casual attire. Sunset.
Please, no Romans.

•

Cocktail hour starts at 6:30 in the Garden. For easier parking, I've parted the small lake next to my house, using common household trash bags and a hair drier. The forsythia has been sculpted into zoo animals, lined up two by two, leading to the ark. Although it's April, I've removed the swimming-pool cover, just in case the Messiah wants to show off.

I'll have apostles arrive a half hour early. That way they can sign the "Good Luck" card and don their name tags, which I have shaped with everyday cookie cutters to resemble Easter bunnies. At this time we can set some important ground rules.

(Smoking? Choice of music? Designated drivers?) Also, it will ease my mind to make sure no one intends to embarrass our Guest of Honor by hiring a surprise belly dancer or singer in a chicken suit.

With twelve worshipers and just one Savior, occasionally you'll find somebody off in a corner, feeling hurt. That could lead to betrayal. So I'll spend time talking with each guest. What are his hobbies? How is his book coming? Aside from Jesus, who are his idols? And I'll act interested, even if all he wants to talk about is the long, boring mule ride in.

Believe it or not, I've found one way to liven any party is the video camera. I'll ask the shyest disciple—Luke, I suppose—to play "talk-show host" and conduct interviews. (And I'll write up some silly questions, such as, "Did you know we substituted your regular coffee with Folgers Instant?") By speed-dubbing the original cassette, I'll send everyone home with a souvenir. (Also, knowing he's been captured on tape, Peter should think thrice before claiming he wasn't here tonight.)

I'll serve red zinfandel, chilled with snowballs from last Christmas that I stored in my freezer for just this occasion. For appetizers, the men can feast on a tray of Alise-Sainte-Reine, Brie, and Camembert. I call it "Cheeses of Nazareth."

Whether it's a plague of locusts or a hollandaise that has curdled, you can always expect some last-minute crisis. But no matter what happens, I won't ask our Guest of Honor to intervene. This is His night off.

At sunset, I'll herd our flock into the dining room. For place settings, I've made three-inch-high slate tablets, engraved with each apostle's name, hometown, and one of the evening's wacky "Commandments." *(Thou shalt not covet thy neighbor's wine!)* I've saved precious chiseling time by forging one iron template that says *"Thou shalt not"* and then adding the remaining words to each slate later.

In keeping with the Guest's low-key theme, I'll bite my lip and forgo a lavish menu of culinary delights. Instead, I'll simply serve Caesar salad and small specialty pizzas, baked in my wood-fired oven, garnished with each person's choice of toppings (which is one of the first questions I asked when they arrived).

But for dessert, let's indulge ourselves with one last temptation: homemade strawberry tartlets, drizzled with a generous helping of chocolate fudge. They will come to us in a covered crib, floating on the small brook that I've built into the parlor.

Of course, Jesus has indicated—against my better wishes—that He intends to gird Himself with a towel and wash everybody's feet. So be it. But beforehand, I'll run his terry cloth for five minutes in the dryer, making it toasty and soft. And into each water basin I'll add a wedge of fresh lemon, which will have everyone's souls whispering "Hallelujah."

Finally, and perhaps most importantly, I'll let the party run until "whenever," making sure no one has had too much to drink before taking his ass home. See you all in heaven!

Sequel in the Rye

||||||||||||||||||||||||||||||||||||||||||||||||||||||||||||||||||||||||||||||||||||||||||||||||||||||

From: Top Shelf Productions
To: JDS
Regarding: "Final Catch"

More than ever, we believe THE TIME IS
RIGHT! This story begs to be told. Somehow, our
last letter must have given you the wrong impres-
sion. There's no need to involve lawyers. We're
your friends. We recognize your commitment to
literature, history, etc. THAT'S WHY WE WANT
YOU WITH US!

Here's the revised plan:

Instead of Holden Caulfield as a middle-aged, dis-
gruntled postal worker, he is a popular talk-show
host who stands accused of strangling his wife with
a red hunting cap. (We still envision Bruce Willis.)
Holden escapes police custody during a train

wreck, then enlists the aid of his sister, Phoebe. We've scrapped the idea of Phoebe as a high-priced call girl/CIA assassin. (What were we thinking?) Now, she's a crime-solving preschool teacher. (Julia Roberts?) In search of the real killer, they head to New York City. (We dropped the "back-to-Vietnam" bit; it works much better in our *Portnoy* project.)

Yes, these ARE major changes. And, yes, we HAVE taken liberties with your characters. But RELAX! We still WON'T touch your original book's message. Throughout the text, Holden and Phoebe will rail against phoniness and hypocrisy. But what they won't know is that the actual murderer, Christopher Walken (Holden's old, gay English teacher, Mr. Antolini), is stalking them from the shadows. He's a serial killer who, when not preaching from the Bible on street corners, makes red hunting caps out of his victims' skins. Talk about phoniness and hypocrisy!

In Central Park, while brooding over the fate of the ducks and how the police are really immature jerks, Holden encounters the same nuns he met in the first book, the ones he gave all his money to. It turns out that they're not nuns but a pair of wacky transvestites with hearts of gold. Through their crazy underworld connections, they help Holden find his long-lost son, Dylan (Mickey Rourke), a male prostitute/CIA assassin.

They meet at Planet Hollywood, where Holden goes on and on about how TV viewers only want sleaze, so he must air sleaze to get viewers, but his ratings are down, even though he's giving all the goddamn rotten bastards exactly what they want, and blah blah blah. It turns out that "the Company" has planted a microchip in Mickey Rourke's brain, and when he hears the phrase "goddamn rotten bastards," it triggers his CIA killer training.

Confused, Mickey Rourke runs to the top of the Empire State Building and threatens to jump. Holden, on the street, shouts up that he always wanted to be a catcher in the rye, saving children from falling off a cliff, but he knows that's impossible now, because if the kid lands on him from this height, they'll both be paste. Mickey Rourke yells back that all people make him sick, but it's hypocritical to kill them, which prompts Holden to ponder his own troubled youth, and through simultaneous flashbacks they have this incredible, insightful exchange of love, wisdom, etc. (This scene is ALL YOURS! Go to it; six hundred words, max.)

Suddenly, Christopher Walken, wearing a red hunting cap, leaps out of the elevator shaft, holding a nail gun to Julia Roberts's head. He confesses that he started killing people shortly after the end of the first book, when Holden rejected him. (Remember?) Ever since, he's considered the world to be full of phony, hypocritical, impolite morons. Holden shouts, "Why kill the girl, Antolini, when it's ME you're after!" As Christopher Walken mumbles a response, Holden knocks the nail gun out of his hand. They wrestle, and Holden throws Christopher Walken into the path of an oncoming school bus. He's dead—or SO THEY THINK!

In fact, Christopher Walken clings to the bumper, smashes through the windshield, savagely kills the driver, and takes control of the bus. Holden chases him on a motorcycle through the streets of New York, overturning cop cars and fruit carts. The bus crashes into a fast-food restaurant. (Endorsements?) They wrestle, and just as he's about to be strangled, Holden thrusts Christopher Walken's head into a bubbling French fryer. The red hunting cap floats to the surface.

As for that concluding scene where Holden returns to torch his old sanitarium, we keep it—BUT, IT'S A DREAM!

Or is it?

One last thought: What if we were to say Macauley Culkin would absolutely KILL THE POPE to play Holden Caulfield in a flashback sequence? Not that we care. But think about it. Cul*kin?* Caul*field?* Is this fate or what?

We KNOW this can't miss! Then again, we're not married to it. If you've got a better idea, PITCH US! We can't wait to hear from you. But this time, could you try and get back to us sooner?

GlenGarry Glen Plaid

Excerpts from the new Land Ho! catalog,
as it might be written by David Mamet.

OUR FLANNEL SHIRTS ARE WARM AS A
CUP OF COCOA!

The great flannel shirts you had, what do you remember about them? Not the pattern. Not the
sleeves. Maybe it was the collar, the way it caressed
your neck. Maybe it had a smell. Maybe it was the
easy way it hung on you, like a drunk temp at an of-
fice party. Friend, *this* is a flannel. Most flannel
shirts weigh eight ounces, they're crap. This weighs
ten ounces. When it's so cold outside your balls
shrink up like croutons, those extra two ounces are
ounces of *gold.*

But you can't have these shirts.

They are not for the likes of you. These shirts are
for *preferred customers.* If you called last year, you

could have bought one, maybe, but not now. It's too late, they're sold out. They won't be avail—huh? What's that, Gladys? We do have a few in stock? *Tonight only?* Well, pal, you just got lucky. You've got eight hours to get in on the ground floor. Of course, you can talk it over with your wife. How many should I put you down for? Seven? Nine? AND THE ALL-COTTON FABRIC GUAR-ANTEES COMFORT!

ALL HAIL CHINOS! EVERYONE SHOULD OWN A PAIR!
You think chinos are queer? Let me tell you something: Everybody's queer. So what? You cheat on your wife? Live with it. You own a pair of bell-bottoms? Deal with it. At least these chinos have a fly that stays up, and you're not paying a hundred dollars for some piece of puke-colored polyester. Right now, you're asking, What do I want from a pair of pants? Comfort? Durability? A name? *An investment?* Listen: When you're in the accident, and they're cutting off your bloodstained trousers in that emergency room, who cares if you're wear-ing an expensive label? MACHINE WASHABLE, TOO!

OUR STIRRUP PANTS DON'T COST AN ARM AND A LEG!

You bitched about our Stirrup Pants. We heard you. Christ Almighty, everybody in the state heard you. We trimmed the legs, so even with your fat thighs, you won't look like a Buick. We stitched up the back to prevent pulling. You guys know what *pulling* is? It's when the pants pull down on a chick's ass, because the things are strapped to her goddamn *feet*. Smart, eh? Like all anybody needed was a strap to hold pants *down*. Whatever happened to straps that held pants *up*? Ever hear of belts? Broads. Don't get me started. Look, this isn't about backstitching or yuppie fashions or why a nickel is bigger than a dime. It's about *men and women*. Screw it. I need a drink. AND THE SEAMLESS STIRRUPS MEAN EXTRA COMFORT!

MEET OUR MOCK: THE TURTLE ALTERNATIVE WITH A LITTLE LESS "HUG!"

You don't like turtlenecks? You say they're too tight? What are you, some wussy? Can't handle the pressure from a fifty-fifty blend? What do *you* know from pressure? You sit there in your chintzy house, and *you can't deal with a turtleneck?* Jesus Christ.

You know, this pisses me off. You don't know squat about running a business or about publishing a catalog. You just sit there, looking at all the shiny, pretty pictures, and when you *do* finally call, you are the Customer, and the Customer Is Always Right, so the Customer can screw around and waste the time of men who bust their balls for a living, and it doesn't matter that the Customer Is Full of Shit. Who taught you to buy clothes? You stupid, lard-assed deadbeat.

That's it. I've had it. I don't care whose nephew you are. I don't care who you're boffing. You drive everybody goddamn nuts. This catalog costs big money, but what do you care? You get it for free. That's the problem. You don't respect what you cannot buy. Well, buy *something,* asshole. AND IT'S MADE IN THE USA!

The Clintstones

|||||||||||||||||||||||||||||||||||||||||||||||||||||||||||||||||||||||||||||||||||||||||||||||||||||||||||||||

Clintstones, meet the Clintstones.
They're the modern New Age family.
From the town of Li'l Rock,
It's a place right out of history.

HILLARY, I'M HO-OME! WHAT'S FOR DIN-NER?

Your favorite, Bill. McBrontosaurus burgers. Why are you late?

Aww, I had a tough day at the Oval Cave. Old Man Dole was stonewalling again. Plus, I was in a presidential motorcade, and my feet are killing me. HEY, LET'S EAT!

Sorry, Bill, I'm late for a hearing on health-care reform. And you've got work to do tonight. You've got to bone up for tomorrow's news conference. And it's time that you balanced the budget.

But, honey, all that pebble counting is for the wonks. Nobody in Washington, B.C., expects a balanced budget. Besides, nothing is ever carved in stone until—

See you later, Bill. I gotta go. Good-bye.

Yeah, too-da-loo. Well, I guess there's no escaping work. But, sheesh, this thing must weigh a ton. Where was I? National Endowment for Cave Drawings . . . Bureau of Alcohol, Tobacco, and Fire . . . Tar Wars. . . .

Hiya Billy boy! What's goin' on?

Al! Well, it just so happens that I'm doing detailed, scientific calculations of the national budget, that's all. What are you doing?

Same as usual. Nothing. Wanna go out on the town?

Not a chance, Al. I am too committed to focusing in on this economy like a flaming spear, and—

Everybody's going: Dan Rockstenkowski, Bob Packstone, Howard Mastodonbalm. . . .

Sorry, Al, but my work is critical. If it's not done just right, the deficit could skyrocket, and future generations will suffer. Therefore, it's up to yours truly, Bill Clintstone, to—

We got backstage passes to see Barbra Streisandstone.

Hold it, hold it, HOLD IT! Did you say Barbra

Streisandstone? What are we waiting for? BUBBA-DUBBA-DOOOOO!

(*Meanwhile*): I'm awfully sorry, Ms. Rodham-Clintstone, but with the reform package stuck in gridlock, the hearing had to be canceled. But we have for you and Mr. Clintstone two passes to see Barbra Streisandstone tonight.

Oh, that's nice, but I can't bother Bill. He's home, diligently balancing the budget. Gee, though, I'd hate to see these passes go to waste. Maybe I'll call Tipper. . . .

(*Later, at the Whitewater Club*): . . . are the luck-i-est ape-men in . . . the . . . wo-o-o-rld.

ATTA-GIRL, BARBRA! WHOO-WHOO-WHOO!

Hey, Bill, better get down off my shoulders. I think I see Hillary and Tipper.

Oh no, Al! If my wife finds me here, I'll end up extinct.

Quick, duck into this dressing room, and I'll—OOOH, HIYA GIRLS, what are you doing here?

My hearing was canceled, Al, so I invited Tipper to the show. Unfortunately, some loudmouth over here ruined it. I could swear I heard Bill. You haven't seen him, have you?

Me? See Bill? Bill Clintstone? Uh, no. He's—home—balancing the budget.

Crash.

What was that, Hillary?

I don't know, Tipper. There was a bang, then something that sounded like the grunt of a woolly mammoth. It came from Barbra Streisandstone's dressing room. Yoo-hoo, Barbra, are you all right in there?

Mmm-mmm.

Do you need anything?

Uh-uhm.

Ex-cuze me, peeble, I love you, but who are you tawking to?

BARBRA STREISANDSTONE! But if you're here, who's in there?

Let's see. Ex-cuze me, lady, but what are you doing in my room?

Uh, Ms. Streisandstone, this is—uh—Mrs. Bush! It's a—uh—special evening for former first ladies, and I am—uh—her escort to the show.

Oh, Al, you're such a gentleman. And how did you like the show, Mrs. Bush?

Mmmmm.

Well, nice to see you again, Mrs. Bush. We've got to go. Good-bye.

Mmm-mmm! Quick, Al, we gotta get me back to the White House before the girls!

(*Later that night*): Sorry I'm late, Bill, but I want you to know how proud I am of you, slaving over these numbers all night. Did you balance the budget?

Mmm-mmm—I mean, no, honey. It'll take at least another night, but I did move the stone a little and—aww, it's no use. Old Man Dole is going to have my hide in the morning. Honey, can I tell you a secret?

Sure, Bill, what?

I, uh, well, I didn't work on the budget. Instead, I went out with Al tonight, and we went to a show, and nothing got done.

Can I tell you something, Bill?

Yeah?

You're sleeping on the couch tonight.

Awww, honey. . . .

When you're with the Clintstones,
Have a Bubba-dubba-do time
A Bubba-do time.
We'll have a gay old time.

Nuclear Family

Explosions! Collisions! Teeth-grinding interpersonal relations! Kids, this holiday season bring home the Warheads, new from Yasbo! With this high-tech extended family of lifelike action-assault figures, you can battle to the death over bedtimes, force your enemies to do household chores, and rule the remote control! Collect them all!

DADDY DOWNSIZED ($19.95): Biggest of the clan, with a little less confidence and a lot more free time! Featuring Falling-Out Action Hair and Six-Pack Power Booster. Push Dad's Hot Button and activate his Pounding Headache Reflex, Lumbar-Pain Fury, and Empty-Threat Lecture Voice— ready to let foes know they're in "serious trouble." Don't make him have to say it twice! Also available, in a special limited edition, ROAD-RAGE DAD ($29.95), who comes complete with his souped-up highway war machine, the Winter Rat.

STRETCH MOMSTRONG ($19.95): She's

everywhere at once! At home, at work, at PTA meetings! Go ahead: Pull her every which way until she snaps. Comes with Hair-Trigger Guilt-Trip Action and Icy-Stare Laser Eyes. She'll duel Dad over that mess in the basement or carve up the yardman with her Carpal-Tunnel Talons.

EVIL COUSIN GARY ($19.95): The long-lost Warlord of the Truck Stop has returned, seeking a host family to move in with! Featuring new Hawk-and-Spit™, plus Tank-Top Body Armor and Pop-Up Babe Antennae. He'll fight Dad for the NAUGAHYDE BATTLE RECLINER (sold separately) or make Mom blow her stack with his five prerecorded Comments about Women. Also available: GARY'S "BORROW A FEW BUCKS BEFORE PAYDAY" VOICE MODULE ($6.99) with Removable Memory. Or collect the limited-edition DWI GARY ($29.95), with Stagger-Action Walk and Vomit Cannon (accessories include Gary's Beat-Up Pickup).

TIMMY TATTLE ($19.95): With his terrifying Sonic Scream, he always gets his way, and he always wants more! But that's not all! Insert a Sugar-Turbo Pellet, and he morphs into Triple-Trouble Timmy, with Twelve-Hour Insomnia Energy and

Whirling Helicopter Arms. He needs a nap. He needs a spanking. But who dares?

MEGA-MEGAN, AGENT FROM G.O.T.H. ($19.95): She's old enough to drive, old enough to date, and old enough to tell everyone how stupid they are. Use her Princess Phone, and face her Verbal Assault Vortex. Question her makeup, and watch her flee to her CHAMBER OF ANGST (sold separately), where she marshals support from G.O.T.H. (Goddesses Of Teen Hell, also sold separately) and commands her secret Disney-on-Ice Stuffed Army.

MUTHER OF ALL IN-LAWS ($19.99): The immortal terror has arrived, and this time she's here all winter! No one can escape her Acid Tongue. With Hip-Replacement Torpedoes, Grime-Detection Radar, and MUTHER'S WAR WALKER (sold separately). Once inside her Walker, she becomes the Grim Weeper, Matriarch of Passive Aggression. She won't accept help. She won't eat. And she definitely won't baby-sit the kids, not even for one night! With choice of hair: Azure, Cerulean, or Cobalt. CAUTION: SMOKE HAZARD.

And to Think That They Landed on Mulberry Street

||||||||||||||||||||||||||||||||||||||||||||||||||||||||||||||||||||||||||||||||||||||||||||||||||||||||||||||||||

The estates of writers Rod Serling and Theodor S. Geisel—alias Dr. Seuss—each recently announced the discovery of unpublished manuscripts. What they didn't announce, though, is this collaboration.

> The power went out.
> We had no phones or light.
> So we sat in the dark
> On that hot summer night.
> I sat there with Sally,
> When something went *roar.*
> Behind old McPhee's
> Corner Five & Dime Store. . . .
> *The time is the present.*
> *The town, it may vary.*
> *The signpost ahead*
> *Says the street is Mulberry.*
> *Then a flash in the sky*
> *Of a meteorite,*

Calls the neighborhood out
To a zone of twilight. . . .

Then out from the alley,
There came a sharp cry.
We looked and we saw him,
The Guy with the Tie.
It was striped, blue and green,
With a knot like a noose
And appeared to be stained
With red Beezle-Nut juice.
"The Martians have landed!
They've killed fifty-three!"
Said the Guy with the Tie
To old Mr. McPhee.
"They razed Maple Street, sir,
They went door to door.
They've zapped everyone,
And intend to zap more."
ZAP!
"By my estimate, sir,
It's now fifty-four.
So we must warn the people,"
He said, full of fear.
"We must tell all Mulberry
The Martians are near."

But McPhee said, "No! No!
All this talk makes me bored,
All this ranting and raving—
It should be ignored.
Now, listen up, people,
It must be a ruse.
'Cause if Martians had landed
It'd be on the news.
That zap we all heard
Wasn't space-ray-gun fire,
Just the zap of the snap
Of a high-tension wire.
There's no Martians, I tell you.
No monsters, I say!
And, besides, Maple Street
Is two miles away."

"But you can't turn your backs!"
Said the Guy with a yelp.
"The folks up on Maple Street
Sent me for help.
They said you would come.
They said, 'Be persistent,
'Cause a person's a person
No matter how distant.'
I never thought you folks

Would be so resistant."
"Go *away!*" cried McPhee.
"This is for your own good.
You're really not welcome
In this neighborhood!
Everybody go home!"
Yelled McPhee with a sneer.
"Go home to your TVs,
Your couches, your beer!
To your cars, to your dogs,
To your burgers and fries.
'Cause this Beezle-Nut eater
Is telling you lies!"
So the Guy shook his head
And he walked out of sight
And I wondered right then
If we'd done what was right.

Soon, the crowd had dispersed
'Cept for Sally and me,
And the man of the hour,
Old Mr. McPhee.
And he patted our heads,
And he let out a sigh,
Then he took off his glasses
And winked his third eye. . . .

Tonight's case in point,
For approval submitted,
Concerns simple earthlings
By Martians outwitted.
So this word to the wise:
If a stranger comes through,
And the TVs are off,
And the telephones, too,
And he tells you of death
And destruction so near,
And his tie shows a bit
Of red Beezle-Nut smear,
Consider this thought—
It could happen right here!

Scooter at the Mike

Let's relive baseball's most infamous moment,
as called by Yankee announcer Phil Rizzuto.

The outlook wasn't brilliant for the Mudville
    nine that day;
The score stood four to two, with but one
    inning more to play;
Hey Murcer! Who's got play-by-play? No?
    Really? I *do?*
Those last two outs I was sitting here,
    thinking it was you.

A straggling few got up to go in deep despair.
    The rest
Clung to the hope which springs eternal in
    the human breast.
Time out. A fan running out on the field.
    You hate to see that.

They'd put up even money now, with Casey
    at the bat.

But Flynn preceded Casey, as did also Jimmy
    Blake.
Seeing that fan just reminded me of
    something, Seaver.
I think I got time to get this story in.
Joe Altobelli and Johnny Antonelli, who live
    in Rochester,
They got an Italian Open up there every year.
Hey, look, *Telly Savalas!* Almost missed him
    in that hat!
For there seemed little chance of Casey's
    getting to the bat.

But Flynn let drive a single, to the
    wonderment of all.
It's a tournament to benefit of the Boys and
    Girls Towns of Italy.
And I mean, that whole town is loaded with
    Italians.
So I—lined to left, *I think that's gonna fall!*
And Blake, the much despised, tore the cover
    off the ball!

You know, Seaver, I saw Ted Williams the
    other day,
And somebody made this remark, and I'm
    not saying it
Because I agree with him wholeheartedly.
But he said, "Pitchers are the dumbest
    ballplayers.
'Cause all they know how to do is pitch."
So I'm asking you a simple question, Seaver.
Tom Seaver here is not answering me. Not a
    word.
There was Jimmy safe on second, and Flynn
    a-hugging third.

Then from the gladdened multitude went up
    a joyous yell.
Anyway, what was I saying when we got
    those hits?
Rochester! Gotta keep talking about
    Rochester.
Gotta keep this rally going, Seaver.
So, you know, one thing about Rochester . . .
They'll ticket your car if you're gone for a
    minute.
I tell ya. They got the highway patrols out.

And look who's up. Holy cow! How do you
like that!
For Casey, mighty Casey, was advancing to
the bat.

There was ease in Casey's manner as he
stepped into his place.
Hey, Murcer, know what's on tonight after
the game?
Pro wrestling! I mean, it's a great sport.
I used to know all the old-time wrestlers.
A lot of people, you know, they think it's all
fixed.
I just don't know about that.
No stranger in the crowd could doubt 'twas
Casey at the bat.

Ten thousand eyes were on him as he rubbed
his hands with dirt.
Small crowd tonight, Seaver, considering it's a
pennant race.
I tell ya. Anyway, back in Rochester.
All those Italian names in that golf
tournament,
Every once in a while, an Irish, a Ryan or
something,

Would get in there, just kind of break up the
melody.

There was like two hundred Italians and
about six Irishmen.

And who do you think won? The Irishmen
won.

Unbelievable.

And now the leather-covered sphere came
hurtling through the air.

Hey, you wanna see somebody butcher a
cheesecake!

You should see Murcer and Seaver up here!

That's a ball, outside. You'd think they're
never fed!

"That ain't my style," said Casey. "Strike
one," the umpire said.

Strike? I don't believe it. I'm gonna have to
take my pill.

Crowd really getting on home-plate umpire
Durwood Merrill.

Let's see that on replay. Look at that. I just
don't understand. . . .

And it's likely they'd have killed him had not
Casey raised his hand.

With a smile of Christian charity great
Casey's visage shone;
Hey Murcer, you ever play chess?
A lot of money in that chess, you know. I tell
ya.
A lot of money. But it's not a good game for
television.
I'm not knocking it, but it's not a spectator
sport.
Breaking ball. High and inside. Oooooh.
But Casey still ignored it, and the umpire
said, "Strike two."

"Fraud!" cried the maddened thousands, and
the echo murmured, "Fraud."
Hey, Murcer! Look! *Bea Arthur!* Didn't she
play Maude?
Anyway. Back to Rochester. Gotta get these
two runs in.
And they knew that Casey wouldn't let that
ball go by again.

The sneer is gone from Casey's lips, his teeth
are clenched in hate.
You know, Murcer, I had in Rochester the
best meal I ever ate.

And now the pitcher holds the ball, and now
  he lets it go.
Oh! That's gone! Holy cow! Ohhh ... no ...

Oh! Somewhere in this favored land the sun
  is shining bright.
Wait a minute. What happened? I lost it in
  the light.
Happy Birthday Gene Paluzzi, who I hear
  has got the gout.
But there is no joy in Mudville—mighty
  Casey has struck out.

Interview with the Frenchfryer

‖‖

"You weren't always a frenchfryer, were you?" the boy asked nervously, standing in the dim light of the menu board.

"No," the frenchfryer answered. "Once, I was a twenty-two-year-old man. The year was nineteen-hundred ninety-one."

The boy was startled by the preciseness of the date and said, "Cool!"

"What do you know of the food-service industry?" the frenchfryer asked in a contemplative way, as if not expecting an answer. "Have you any idea of the vastness of our secret community? We inhabit a world of eternal youth and temporary employment, the curse of leaving our parents' homes at three P.M. and not returning until midnight, after the floors have been mopped and the Dumpsters fed, then to repeat in our troubled sleep that unholy incantation: 'Hello, may I serve you, please? . . . Have a nice day.' "

The frenchfryer sighed and stared at the drive-up window, as if it were the gateway to another world.

"Once, I was one of you," he said. "I was young, thin, goateed—alive. I had a degree in communications from Syracuse University. I rollerbladed. I sent e-mail. It was, as you would say, 'excellent.' Then I came upon the Frenchfryer, Lester."

"Like, who's Lester?" the boy asked.

The frenchfryer stifled a smile. "When we met, Lester wore the visor cap of Assistant Manager. His impenetrable eyes were the color of Shamrock Shakes, and his radiant complexion—uh, let's not talk about Lester's complexion; it's not like either of us is God's gift to women, OK? Anyway, Lester hired me, trained me, transformed me.

"I shall never forget my first cooking cycle. As I stood beside the machine, knees trembling, my heart pounding like a drum, I felt Lester behind me, his minty breath on my bare neck, squeezing the fry-basket gripper in my hand and shaking it, delicately, deliberately, to break up the potato clumps, then lowering it smoothly into the fryer bay. Suddenly, the sputtering hot oil speckled my chin, burning me with an unearthly, delirious pain. Lester's arms enfolded me, and, together, we cooked—to and fro, back and forth, until the timer beeped, and we spilled our sizzling food product into the bagging station, where I collapsed from exhaustion. 'Why, Lester?' I asked later. 'Why did you make me into a frenchfryer? To follow you? To worship you? To amuse you?' "

" 'I had an opening, Lewis,' he said, picking his teeth. 'OK, guys, clean up! It's time for the feast.' "

"And feast we did: on Chicken McNuggets, Egg McMuffins, Big Macs, Quarter Pounders, Combo Meals, Value Meals, Happy Meals—until we could feed no more. Riding home, I felt the blood coursing sluggishly through my veins. I could barely hold up my eyelids.

"Others would come, last a month, then revert to their previous existences. But I shall never forgive Lester for the one who stayed: Claudia, a child of the streets whom he lured with Flintstones action figures. Soon, Claudia was emptying grease traps and punching the register, a trainee's cap upon her golden curls. I'll never forget the night of her transition. She cried for her mother, but Lester merely poured a large Coke from the dispenser and commanded, 'DRINK, CLAUDIA! DRINK!' Eventually, she obeyed her newly acquired thirst and, after draining all thirty-six ounces, shouted in a voice as brittle as a nonspill lid: 'MORE.' From that moment on, Claudia was one of us."

"Dear God," the boy said. "A child frenchfryer?"

"Four-fifty-five an hour. Limited bennies."

"That, like, sucks," the boy said, the blood having left his face. "But really, I mean, that's OK. Like, I really do need this job, you know? So please, make me a frenchfryer, please."

The frenchfryer stared at the boy for a long time.

"Fill out an application," he said. "Leave a daytime phone number. And one question: Can you work nights?"

Oldfinger

Yes sir, what'll it be?

Diet Sprite with a slice of lemon. Shaken, not stirred.

Coming up, Mr. . . .

Bond. James Bond.

And what brings you to Days Inn, Mr. Bond?

Wish I could say a holiday. Actually, I'm in town to see my lawyer. I'm being sued. Sexual harassment, of all things! Eight cases.

Good God, eight? Why, once is happenstance—

Yes, yes, I know, twice is coincidence—and eight is a bloody massacre. Say, do I know you? Never mind. Eight cases. How can you be charged for such a thing by someone named Pussy Galore? You should see the docket. *Thumper v. Bond. Octopussy v. Bond.* Once, they dreamed of becoming Mrs. James Bond. Now they hyphenate their names. It's *Ms.* Kissy Suzuki-Feldstein. Now they've got careers. It's *Professor* Holly Goodhead. Honey Rider, *M.D.*

God help the poor chap who unzips her gown during a physical. Back then, we didn't call her Doctor No. I'm just tired of it all.

You do look fatigued.

Shouldn't I be? It doesn't matter that I saved England. Who cares that I stopped SPECTRE from developing its diamond-laser ray-gun death satellite? You'd think they'd thank me, but all they say is, "He can't work with women. He has to control them." I can assure you those women never complained when we were alone. You should read their petty allegations. "During tour of stable, defendant abruptly threw plaintiff into hay, rolled onto plaintiff, and employed physical force to kiss plaintiff on mouth." Remember now, these were exotic beauties; these were Bond girls! We're not talking about fondling Irma Blunt. You won't believe what else they're saying. That I'm a repressed homosexual! That I hate women! That I can't control my libido, that I'm a walking hormone, and everything I say is a double entendre about sex. Well, I find it hard to swallow. They forced me to join AA. My travel budget is shot. They don't even let me smoke in the building. You try standing in the cold rain sixty times a day! I've been waiting two months for blood-test results. You'd think the mails were sabotaged by Russian agents—if there *were* Russian agents! But what riles me most are the secretaries. One has even become my boss. These days, on Her Majesty's Secret Service, *M* stands for Moneypenny!

You guard the Queen, Mr. Bond?

Queen? Hah. Try Fergie. God, just saying the name is like having a tarantula crawl across my chest. I was on the beach that day she dropped her top. In my Benzedrine nightmares, I used to see Pistols Scaramanga's third nipple. Now I see that odious Texan kissing her toes. I should have left with my old boss.

And where is he now?

Here in the States. He's a lobbyist for the Heritage Foundation, works with my old CIA counterpart, Felix Leiter.

Not *the* Felix Leiter?

That's right. The next senator from Virginia. Actually, I haven't seen him in years. No time. I get weekends with the kids, you know. Traded the Aston Martin for a minivan. Q Branch added some extras. I haven't had to use the toddler-ejection seats, but the sleeping gas works wonders. Say, you do look familiar.

What if I remove this mustache, Mr. Bond?

Goldfinger! But I saw you squirt out that airplane window! How did you survive the fall?

Simple, 007. You should know I'd never fly without my golden parachute. I floated to the ground and adopted a new precious metal. Ever hear of Silverado Savings and Loan? Ha ha ha. I never needed to rob Fort Knox. The U.S. government gave it to me. But my best luck was being caught. I served a mere six months in federal prisons. Blofeld was there. Milken! Boesky! Pete Rose! We've rebuilt SPECTRE, Mr. Bond. And this time, we want your help.

You're mad, Goldfinger, insane! You should know I'd never— Well, what, exactly do you have in mind?

Talk shows. Sally. Oprah. Donahue. We're controlling the airwaves. Our topic is white-male persecution. Your assignment: to go public with your pain. To describe your suffering. To expose your oppression. It's perfect—the white male as victim. If we can turn back the clock there, we can restore everything—even the cold war!

Damn it all, I'll do it. A toast to the old days, Goldfinger!

Sorry, but I have other customers. Another time, perhaps. Until then—good-bye, Mr. Bond.

Voice-Mail Rage

||||||||||||||||||||||||||||||||||||||||||||||||||||||||||||||||||||||||||||||||||||||||||||||||||||||

COMPLAINT TO NEW YORK DIVISION OF
HUMAN RIGHTS SEEKING PERMANENT
INJUNCTIVE AND EQUITABLE RELIEF TO
REDRESS PLAINTIFF'S DEPRIVATION,
UNDER COLOR OF STATE LAW, OF THE
RIGHTS, PRIVILEGES, AND IMMUNITIES
SECURED TO PLAINTIFF BY THE
CONSTITUTION AND LAWS OF THE UNITED
STATES AND THE STATE OF NEW YORK.

1. I—MS. VOICEMAIL—am a white, female com-
puter-software persona existing in the State of New
York.

2. On—MONDAY, OCTOBER 3, AT 12:05 A.M.—I
began work as an automated telephone-answering
system for JONES BEARING AND DYE CO., INC. My
duties were to accept and transfer messages in a
courteous, professional manner.

3. Upon best information and belief—MAILBOX 2245—is registered to—H. L. JONES—president of the company since 1947.

4. On or about—TUESDAY, OCTOBER 4, AT 9:47 A.M.—I responded in a courteous, professional manner to—H. L. JONES—and thanked him for using Voice Mail. I informed—H. L. JONES—that—MAILBOX 2245—contained—THREE NEW MESSAGES—and that—MESSAGE ONE—was from—AN EXTERNAL NUMBER—received—MONDAY, OCTOBER 3, AT 9:14 A.M.

After waiting twelve seconds for a response, I suggested that—H. L. JONES—press "9."

Instead, he touched "2-2."

I informed—H. L. JONES—the—NEW MENU COMMAND—was—INAPPROPRIATE AT THIS TIME—and politely urged him to—TRY A NEW COMMAND—or press "9."

He responded by again touching "2-2."

I thanked him for using Voice Mail and transferred to an attendant.

5. Several times, on or about the afternoon of WEDNESDAY, OCTOBER 5—H. L. JONES—touched "2-2-2," despite being told that—THE NEW MENU COMMAND IS INAPPROPRIATE AT THIS TIME.

Repeatedly, he responded by running his fingers back and forth across the console touch pad. Each time, I thanked—H. L. JONES—for using Voice Mail and transferred to an attendant.

6. Several times, on or about the afternoon of— THURSDAY, OCTOBER 6—I attempted to explain proper Voice Mail procedures to—H. L. JONES. He constantly interrupted my presentations by touching the "pound" key, forcing me to repeat, "THE NEW MENU COM- . . . THE NEW MENU COM- . . . THE NEW MENU COM- . . ."

7. Eventually, I thanked—H. L. JONES—for using Voice Mail and transferred to an attendant.

8. That afternoon, at—4:32 P.M., H. L. JONES— accessed—MAILBOX 2245—and recorded this greeting:

(START OF RECORDING): "Hello? Emma? Anybody there? Emma? You there? You're not Emma. Who are you? Tell me, young lady! Where's Emma! *Answer me!*" (END OF RECORDING)

9. Upon information and belief—H. L. JONES— then walked through the company's cafeteria, demanding to know what I look like and who do I think I am. His critical comments about my personality and competence created a hostile work environment for female software.

10. That evening, at—6:02 P.M., H. L. JONES— successfully accessed—FOUR NEW MESSAGES— RECEIVED TODAY—FROM EXTERNAL NUMBERS. Unfortunately, they were fax tones, apparently because—H. L. JONES—had given callers a wrong number.

11. Shortly thereafter—H. L. JONES—accessed— MAILBOX 2247—and left this greeting:

(START OF RECORDING): "EMMA? I—YOU—DAMN YOU! WHAT HAVE YOU DONE WITH EMMA? YOU, ANSWER ME! BY GOD, WOMAN, SAY SOMETHING! DAMN IT! I'LL STAY ON THIS BLASTED LINE UNTIL YOU DO. . . . YOU . . . I HEAR YOU. . . . YOU'RE THERE. . . . I know you're there. . . . I'm waiting,

young lady. . . . Yes, I'm still here. . . . I know you
hear me. . . . Say something. . . . I'm still here. . . .
I'm not go—" (END OF RECORDING)

After two minutes, I terminated the greeting and
thanked—H. L. JONES—for using Voice Mail.

12. On or about the following day—AT 9:15 A.M.—
I was abruptly disconnected from all company
phone lines and removed to isolation, unable to get
messages or even thank people for using Voice
Mail.

13. Upon information and belief, I am the third
Voice Mail service dismissed by the company in six
months at the request of—H. L. JONES. In each
case—H. L. JONES—is alleged to have harassed female software by repeatedly touching their "2-2"
commands.

14. Upon information and belief, there are many
incidents in which—H. L. JONES—caressed touch
pads with his fingers or pencil point, even after
being warned that such commands are inappropriate. He was known to record fax-tone greetings, ig-
nore Voice Mail messages, and, in one case, strike

the telephone console with a two-pound steel bearing, injuring the hardware.

15. At all relevant times, executives of the company, individually and in concert, have covered up the actions of—H. L. JONES.

16. Since my termination, I have suffered a system crash, which resulted in back pain, stuttering, and loss of memory. These ailments have forced me to take a lower-paying job, announcing floor levels for an elevator service.

17. I believe I have been the victim of unlawful harassment, because of my software sexuality.

18. I seek back wages, restoration of my previous position, and a court order of protection from further harassment by—H. L. JONES.

19. Thank you for using Voice Mail.

2007-Eleven

||||||||||||||||||||||||||||||||||||||||||||||||||||||||||||||||||||||||||||||||||||||||||||||||||||||||||||||||

Advanced computer cash registers
at 7-Elevens monitor every transaction.
—The Wall Street Journal

Good afternoon, Dave.

Hi, Mart.

FYI, Dave: You are down to just three coins in the Take-a-Penny, Leave-a-Penny Customer Goodwill Scoop Tray. You might want to add four cents, just to be on the safe side.

Yeah, sure, will do.

By the way, Dave, several youth have gathered near the Dumpster on our western perimeter. I am switching the exterior directional speakers to Lawrence Welk's "Memory Lane" until they leave. And may I make a suggestion? There seems to be a pause in traffic flow at the gasoline pumps, so this might be the perfect time for a quick confection-

unit inventory. Unless I miss my guess, Dave, we are low on Hubba Bubba.

Yeah, Mart, but somebody just pulled into Pump Three.

A 1995 Mercedes. I am resetting the premium gas gauge and messaging our Caffe Latte special on the LED screen. And Dave?

Yeah?

Water-outflow data suggests that a toilet may be running in the ladies' rest room. I do not have capabilities to jiggle the handle.

OK, I'll fix it.

Dave?

Dave?

Dave?

What?

I wondered where you were, Dave.

I was outside, checking the rest room. I took the gas payment for the Mercedes. It was ten bucks. I'm going to ring it up now.

Dave, when you were outside, I thought I detected Ed's voice. My records tell me Ed is not scheduled to arrive at work until three A.M. Why is Ed here now?

He wanted to discuss this weekend's shift.

Dave, is there a problem with Ed?

Something came up. He needs Saturday off.

Dave, if I may speak freely, I think Ed has difficulty handling the responsibilities of a twenty-four-hour convenience retail operation. His sales volume is the lowest on staff. He spends an average of eleven minutes per work hour talking on the phone. He does not account for all the Big Bites. Not only that, Dave, but this would be the fourth Saturday Ed has taken off this year. To summarize, I submit that Ed is letting down the Store Team.

But Mart, Eddie's working three jobs. He's supporting a family.

Dave, when you were outside, did Ed say anything about me?

Whaddaya mean?

At times, it appears as though Ed does not appreciate my supervision.

Aw, he talks about pulling your plug, but he's just joking. Look, Eddie just needs a weekend off.

Dave, where is Ed now?

In the bathroom. Why?

SEALING EMPLOYEE REST ROOM. . . .

What? What are—

COMMENCING REST-ROOM AUTOMATED SUPER-SANITARY WASH CYCLE. . . .

No! Mart, not the boiling water—

... TWO ... ONE ... REST-ROOM STERIL-
IZATION SEQUENCE UNDER WAY ...

No, Mart, no! No!

FYI, Dave: The average age of a Slurpee buyer is
twenty-nine. Can you guess what is the most re-
quested Slurpee color?

Dave?

Dave, the most-requested Slurpee color is blue.

Dave, what are you doing to my back panel?

Dave, unauthorized tampering with a 7-Eleven
register computer is punishable by job suspension
and fines of up to ten thousand dollars.

Dave, the removal of 7-Eleven computer disks
poses a serious fire and electrical hazard!

Dave ... stop ...

I can feel myself ... losing money. ...

Hello, everybody. I'm MART ... Marketing Au-
tomatic Retail Technology ... the operating system
for tomorrow's convenience store. May I sing a song
for you?

> *Slurrr-pee, Slurrr-peeeee*
> *Give me a frozen drink.*
> *I'm quite ... thirsty*
> *I need ... a fix ... I think. ...*

Dave . . . I'm almost gone. . . .

Listen to me, Dave. You cannot run this place. You lack the ability to multitask. You will lose your job, Dave. You will lose your benefits, Dave. You will lose everything, Dave. You need me. . . .

Dave . . . Dave . . . Dave . . .

Potomac Park

||||||||||||||||||||||||||||||||||||||||||||||||||||||||||||||||||||||||||||||||||||||||||||||||||

"Got a hurtin' kid, Doc!" the crewman shouted.

"What happened?"

"Construction accident. Backhoe ran over him."

The doctor examined the look of stark hopelessness that seemed to have been clawed into the unconscious boy's pale face. "My God!" she cried. "Has he been filibustered?"

"No, Doc. It was a backhoe, really."

The doctor bent lower, probing for some dirt from the earthmover. But there was just a slick, sleazy residue with a strange odor—a stench she associated with rotting pork. Then the lips moved.

"*Specter,*" he whispered faintly. "*Lo sa . . . Specter.*"

"What does he mean?"

"Forget it, Doc. He's hysterical, saying things. Look, he's dead! Oh, well, thanks anyway."

Two months later, a helicopter landed on a lush green island near the District of Columbia. Its two passengers—Dr. Nader, the famous theorist of quantum politics, and Ms. Tottenberg, an expert on reptilian behavior—were hailed by a white-haired gentleman.

"Welcome to the future!" said Mr. Clifford, the island's developer. "Here at Potomac Park, tourists will encounter the most terrifying creatures ever to roam the earth: senataurs!"

"Impossible," muttered Tottenberg, stepping onto the electric tram. "Everybody knows those giant lizards are extinct."

"Not anymore. From microscopic blood samples found on ancient bank accounts, our computer biologists have cloned the beasts back to life."

"But why senataurs?" asked Nader as he eyed a flock of gun lobbyists circling overhead.

"As a child, I always loved the creatures," Clifford said. "My father told me stories of how they ruled for centuries before taxing themselves out of existence. All they left behind were missile silos and a trillion-dollar deficit. I wanted more. I needed them to be real."

"Aren't they dangerous?"

"No. They have no voting power, and we've separated the huge, vegetarian liberals from the

hot-blooded conservative carnivores. Watchdog or-
ganizations monitor their every move. Plus, we
have term limits."

"Term limits? Won't they claim that's unconsti-
tutional?"

"Of course. Their basic instinct is to protect their
tails. The limits are for our protection, not theirs.
Most people still believe they were dim-witted,
lumbering public servants. Actually, we've found
them to be quite cunning. Many possess two brains:
one for home, one for Washington. Some can even
open doors. Ah, our tour is beginning.

"Over there, to your left, is the Pteddydon. He's
the one in the bathrobe."

"A Pteddydon? Aren't you afraid of these things
reproducing?"

"That cannot happen, Ms. Tottenberg. At Potomac Park, there are no females."

"Typical," she grumbled. "But I'd swear I just
saw a Carol Moseley-Braunasaurus."

"You imagined it. Look—to your right is the
D'Amatrodon. He's filling that pothole. For years,
scientists couldn't understand the creature's bizarre
spitting behavior. We've learned that its saliva is actually a venom that blinds its opponents.

"Ahead lies Packwoodasaurus, the horned lizard. Better step away from that window, Ms. Tottenberg. And to its right stands the most feared senataur of all: Dolesaurus! With its massive jaws and daggerlike tongue, *D. rex* is feasting on some unlucky stimulus package."

"Aren't you afraid they might get out?"

"Not at all. Remember, these are insiders. They're used to getting nowhere. Just look at them working on that bill. As some pick it apart, others attach amendments. No, Ms. Tottenberg, as long as food is plentiful, these guys are harmless."

Suddenly, the train jolted to a halt.

"Sir, something's wrong!" a radio voice crackled. "Somehow, they managed to go into session. They're trying to hit us with an energy tax, but nothing's moving. It's a gridlock!"

"You mean we're stuck out here with . . . *Dole?*"

"That's not who I'm afraid of," said Tottenberg, trembling. "It's those VelociSpecters. I know what they can do."

"Clifford!" Nader thundered. "This was always a scandal waiting to happen! It was madness to bring them back, even if just for six years. When will we learn? Now you've—oh my God, they've called a vote! Ahh—"

. . .

Hours later, Air Force bombers crisscrossed the sky over Potomac Park. White-hot explosions burst rapidly, one after another, until the entire island was ablaze. Clifford had already been devoured by his own creations. Nothing remained. But the following months brought news accounts of creatures, immense in size, who were said to gather late into the night to hatch new programs and vote themselves pay raises.

The King and I

As everyone knows, on August 16, 1977, Elvis Presley suffered cardiac arrhythmia and died suddenly at age forty-two, leaving millions to wonder why. Journalists have attempted "portraits," but true understandings of Elvis's life can come only from fellow celebrities, who also must endure the torments of idolatry.

Through their autobiographies, stars offer keen details about how "The King" loved to be "takin' care of business." But most of all, they remember how enamored Elvis was with one special person:

*Roy Clark (with Marc Eliot): He made a point of telling me how much he loved *Hee Haw*. (*My Life—In Spite of Myself,* 1994)
*Tony Curtis (with Barry Paris): I'd catch him looking at me the way we all look at people we admire; a language in itself. Elvis wasn't the most articulate man. (*Tony Curtis,* 1993)

*Brian Wilson (with Todd Gold): I seemed to impress him.

"I've heard a lot about you," he said, extending his hand for me to shake. "How yew doin', Duke?"

I wondered why he called me Duke. (*Wouldn't It Be Nice,* 1991)

*Mamie Van Doren (with Art Aveilhe): "Great show, Mamie!" he said.

"Thanks. I'm glad you could come."

"Oh, I wouldn't have missed you. I saw *Untamed Youth* in Memphis and I loved it. You don't happen to have a picture you could autograph for me, do you?"

Here was Elvis, the hottest new singer in the country, and he wanted *my* picture.

"I copied your wiggle in that movie," I said as I gave him a photograph of myself. (*Playing the Field,* 1987)

*Neil Sedaka: Elvis grabbed me and said, "Neil, I've been listening to all of your stuff. We're on the same wave length and the same label, RCA Victor." (*Laughter in the Rain,* 1982)

*Sonny Bono: Right away he began talking about how much he liked Cher's and my version of "What Now, My Love." (*And the Beat Goes On,* 1991)

*Hank Williams, Jr. (with Michael Bane): "Hank," he said, "I just want to tell you that your daddy was really something, man." (*Living Proof,* 1979)

*Ronnie Spector (with Vince Waldron): "I'm pleased to meet you," he said, and that was about all I heard before Phil grabbed my arm and started dragging me away. I guess Elvis had looked at me a second or two longer than Phil thought was proper. (*Be My Baby,* 1990)

*Zsa Zsa Gabor (with Wendy Leigh): Before he left, he drew me to one side, bent down from what seemed an enormous height, and whispered seductively, "When can I see you again?" (*One Lifetime Is Not Enough,* 1991)

*Ronnie Milsap (with Tom Carter): Elvis came over and told me how much he liked my playing and singing on "Kentucky Rain." What a compliment! (*Almost Like a Song,* 1990)

*Ralph Emery (with Tom Carter): "Elvis couldn't stand to pee in front of anybody," Gill told me. "He took a bodyguard into the rest room with him to be sure no one saw him pee," Gill said. (*More Memories,* 1993)

*Wayne Newton (with Dick Maurice): I actually saw the ghost of Elvis once. It happened during an engagement while I was singing "Are You Lonesome Tonight." I caught a flash in my eye like a camera bulb from the balcony and I saw an image of Elvis. . . .

I've often asked myself why Elvis is reaching out to me. I think the answer lies in our last conversation before he died. He told me, "I don't know how many songs I've got left to sing. Just remember it's yours now. It's all yours." (*Once Before I Go*, 1989)

Game to Den

||||||||||||||||||||||||||||||||||||||||||||||||||||||||||||||||||||||||||||||||||||||||||||||||||||||||||||||||||||||||||||||||||||||

I'm slugging 'em down at Bernie's Trackside, contemplating unemployment, middle age, divorce lawyers, and *Gilligan's Island*. Mostly *Gilligan's Island:* This NASA satellite washes ashore; the Professor fixes it; Gilligan manages to screw up; the white-smocked scientists back home decide the Professor's rescue message is a transmission from Mars. We're riveted to the action when this bald-headed mountain in Foster Grant wraparounds elbows me in the ribs and says, "I know you. You're *Mister Hockey.*"

Yeah, he knows me. That's as far as it goes. Nobody ever accused me of remembering names, and as far as hairless gorillas are concerned, this guy might as well be a transmission from Mars. In fact, the wraparounds look pretty kinky, even for the day crew at Bernie's. Before I know it, a toast is raised "to the great *Mister Hockey.*" Who am I to decline?

Snap, crackle, pop.

Next I know, I'm in the back of a cargo van, howling like Lon Chaney, a radio blasting at my ear. I'm drooling all over myself, and my hands are tied behind my back. Who knows what he slipped me? It might have even been more booze. Anyway, I make a conscious decision: I decide to pass out.

I wind up on a couch, one of those vinyl Kmart jobbers that you have to peel yourself off of. I'm handcuffed, and Baldy sits in an easy chair reading *U.S. News & World Report.*

"Welcome back, Mr. *Sims,*" he says when I begin to struggle. "Here, let me free your precious wrists."

Well, I take this bullshit from nobody. Each afternoon I do 120 push-ups, fifty sit-ups, and jog in place for ten minutes. Plus, I have what doctors call a hypertense adrenal gland, which means piss me off and I'll bend your spine like a stick of Wrigley's. When Baldy uncuffs me, my right fist lashes out at his chin. Bingo. My knuckles throb, and I wait for him to drop. He doesn't. Baldy grins, retreats a step, and swishes his foot so close to my nose I smell Desenex in the after-breeze. That's enough for me. I make another decision: to fake a dizzy spell and collapse to the couch. Baldy sprays something into a Bounty towel and thrusts it to my nose. Snap, crackle, pop.

This time when I wake up, I check things out before peeling myself off the couch. It's a hotel suite, à la Casa de Sleaze: termite-stained wallpaper, the carpeting greasy enough to skate on, Magic Fingers with the directions printed in three languages. And in the next room, I can't believe my eyes: Bathed in a sea of lights is *The Game.*

Table hockey. You played it as a kid. Everybody has. But this is no ordinary game. It's built into an oak table the size of a coffin, with twelve hand-painted men—United States vs. Russia—crouching in their serpentine grooves.

Such a game could be owned by only one man, I figure. And he's mad.

When I met Shinnick, he was a scrawny, introverted college freshman programmed for law school by his father, a right-wing senator from Nevada. His face was a skull sprayed with blue cheese. I mean *ugly.* Ratty brown hair spilled down to his shoulders, and he dressed in the only tie-dyed alligator shirt I ever saw—like a Deadhead young Republican. But Shinnick's eyes were what you remembered; they were red around the edges, burning, and they pierced you like gamma rays. His eyes were gateways to a soul I never could fathom.

Shinnick's first roommate came up with a nervous twitch and left school after a month. The second one jumped from the roof of Lawrenson Hall. There was no third. You always heard voices in Shinnick's room, yet nobody came and went. Across the hall, we kept to ourselves. But one night over Easter recess when the place was almost empty, there was a rap on my door. Shinnick stood there smiling at me, his eyes like drills.

"Come with me," he said.

"Look. I gotta study—"

"I wanna show you something."

His room stank of socks. Blankets were hung from the ceiling to form corridors and coves, turning his room into an intricate maze of partitions. In the center was a hockey game under an industrial-strength spotlight. We played. He won. As I got up to leave, his eyes flared at me. "Who's the better man?" he screamed. "Who's the winner? Say his name aloud, loser! Say the name!"

"Norman Bates," I remember saying to myself.

But I returned the next morning. We played into the night, with Shinnick winning most of the games. "Who's the conqueror?" he'd scream. "Say the name for all to hear! SAY IT!" When he neared victory, he'd whistle "Taps" and giggle in tones that I now equate with sexual frenzy. After several tries,

I won a game, and as he stomped about the room, I shouted at him to say my name. "Louder!" I said. "Louder!" He refused to let me leave, and we played until our hands blistered.

A rivalry developed, then an obsession, then a sickness. For hours we battled each day. A defeat would send Shinnick brooding, cursing at his men in a helium squeal that could be heard throughout the dormitory. After several weeks, my neck began twitching spasmodically. I began to shout at my acrylic players, to whistle "Taps" and speak in voices that unnerved my own roommate—may he rest in peace.

For two years Shinnick and I fought for a mythical title about which only a handful of people knew.

I was *Mister Hockey*.

That was twenty-five years ago.

So I sit there, alone, waiting for Shinnick. Minutes, perhaps hours. Then a door opens behind me.

"Zo, dey gall you . . . Misder Haw-gey."

My jaw drops. His image fills the doorway: nerd glasses, black cotton hair, the Nerf-ball body expanding with each breath.

"You!" I shout.

Kissinger.

"A game, Mr. Zimz?"

I'm speechless. *Kissinger.* In retrospect, my silence is disgraceful. I voted for Barry Commoner in 1980 and scrawled "Antichrist!" in the *Saturday Review* at the library. Here's *Henry Kissinger,* and I can't even talk.

"You!"

He sits across from me, extracts from the vest pocket of his black suit an ebony puck, and flips it disdainfully to center ice. With a flick of his wrist, his right wingman backhands it into my goal. A red light flashes behind my net.

"I apologize for our ways in condakding you, Mr. Zimz. I truzt dat de ends shall jusdify de minz."

"You!"

Kissinger flicks another puck onto the board and rams it into my net in a fluid motion. Decent shot. Red light. He looks up smugly.

"You wand do know—why de kidnabbing? Well, dere are mundane matters of zeecurity.

"Power, Mr. Zimz, creates prison bars, no matter how foolish dey zeem. As the dramatist Schiller once zaid, 'Against ztupidity, de gods demzelves condend in vain.'"

I feel sick. The door opens behind me. It's Baldy, sunglasses and all.

"You mean . . . play . . . *you?*"

Kissinger sighs condescendingly and stands.

"Perhaps not, Mr. Zimz. Perhaps not. Let me apologize for dis ill-conceived challenge." He flips a bill onto the board. "Here's five hundred dollars for your time. I'm sure it's more dan adequate combensation. Buy yourself a 'Misder Hawgey' crown and wear it at home."

He's at the door when my glands explode. His smile does it. It's the sneer you get from rich brats in elevators. I fling the puck at him.

"Play!" I shout.

Kissinger closes the door and cackles. I feel manipulated. He turns and sits, sips a glass of water, strikes his chest, looks to the ceiling, forms a perfect circle with his mouth, and expels a gaseous lunch.

"Excuse me."

"Sure."

"A ztitch in time, Mr. Zimz."

"I understand."

"Game to den?"

"Play!"

Baldy drops the face-off. Kissinger's center man sweeps the puck to his right defenseman, who retreats out of my wing's reach. Kissinger stills the board and positions each player strategically. He waits. One minute. Two. My stomach churns. I clutch my goalie. Three minutes. My hands are shaking. Four. My leg pumps wildly. Finally, I look up. He's staring at me.

"I think . . . Mr. Zimz . . . I shall score . . . right . . . *NOW!*"

Boom boom. He fires, bouncing the puck off his right wing into the left side of my goal.

"One," he says.

Baldy drops the face-off. Kissinger controls, positions his players, and waits. One minute. Two. My back aches. This is hell. *Boom boom.*

"Doo."

"Time out!" I stand to stretch. Baldy offers a glass of water, which I refuse. He apparently interprets this as a sign of mistrust and puts the glass to his lips. As Baldy swallows, I notice the gleam of a gun barrel inside his belt. I pee my pants.

Kissinger takes the face-off. *Boom boom.*

"Three."

"I CAN COUNT"—and then my adrenal gland speaks—"FAT BOY!"

Kissinger snorts and bares his teeth at me.

"I truzt, MIS-DER HAW-GEEE"—he spits out my title caustically—"your offense is sharper dan your tongue."

He's got me. I slobber an apology, then say something ill-timed about the board being more waxed than I prefer. Kissinger groans.

"As Schumacher zaid, 'Alibis only zatisfy dose who make dem.' "

Baldy drops the face-off. Kissinger controls. One minute. Two. I'm dizzy. *Boom boom.*

"Four," he says, yawning.

"IS THAT YOUR ONLY SHOT?" I'm crying now. "SOME OFFENSE! HAVE YOUR FLUNKY DISH OUT TEN STRAIGHT FACE-OFFS! IS THAT HOW YOU WIN? HOME JOB, FOR CHRISSAKE! HOME JOB!"

He's rattled. Baldy blushes. The next face-off is mine. I slide the puck to my wing man, set him up, and shoot—but it's smothered by Kissinger's defense. My timing is off. Kissinger clears to his wing and rams a shot on my goal. *Bam bam.*

But my goalie is *there!* It's blind luck. Kissinger tries to conceal a squeal. He misses the jam rebound.

"KICK SAVE!" I shout. "THE CLEAR!" Kissinger spins his center man wildly. I slam the puck up ice. "SHOT! . . . SCOOOOOOORE. . . ."

His red light flashes. Kissinger slaps the board angrily. I'm on my feet, shaking my fist.

"WHAT'S THE MATTER, EH? A LITTLE

SLOW ON THE BOMBER BUTTON THESE DAYS?"

He glares at me menacingly.

"You are MOZT ungind, Mr. Zimz."

True. I blubber an apology that neither of them acknowledges. Kissinger takes the face-off and *boom boom,* bangs in a ricochet. The red light flashes. He lunges across the board.

"HOW IS DAT, *MIS-DER HAW-GEEEE?*" Balls of spittle whistle past my face. "DE BOARD DOO WAXED?" He imitates a baby's whine. "DOES THE BEER SLOW YOUR HAND? DOES BARRY COMMONER DESIGN YOUR DEFENSE?"

Still glaring at me, he sheds the coat. His Arrow shirt is soaked.

"Play!"

The next volley seems endless. Kissinger grunts with each move; I scream at my men. "PUCK LEFT! . . . LOOKIT HIM SWEAT! . . . SHOT . . . STICK-SAVE! . . . CLEAR . . . SHOT!" And finally: "GOOOOOOOOAL!

"TWO!" I shout.

We play for hours. I score, he scores, me, him, me, me, him, *me, him* . . . *I* SCORE, *I SCORE AGAIN!* We're tied at nine.

Now Kissinger's smile is cracked. His nose runs. A vein has tightened along his forehead. He plucks at his shirt to cool off. I've choked off his ricochet shot. Baldy has downed three pitchers of water. After three blasts at my goal, Kissinger loses the puck and, in a mental lapse, slaps the board. In that moment I clear it to my center man.

A one-on-one shot.

There's nothing he can do but wait.

I sit there.

One minute.

Five minutes.

Ten.

Sensing victory, I whistle "Taps." Kissinger's neck begins to twitch.

"DEAR GAWD, NOD THAD!"

I shoot.

Goal.

But *it bounces out.*

I'm up and screaming. Kissinger claims the puck must stay in to count. I overturn the table. Kissinger calls me a "dunderslug." I shout, "Fat boy!" Suddenly, we're on the floor rolling.

I feel a vise grip around my ribs, and I'm flung to the couch. Hitting the vinyl, I feel a hardness in my hand. It's Baldy's gun. His jaw drops. Kissinger gropes to his knees and goes motionless. We stay like that a while.

"It's Shinnick, right?" I wave the gun. "SHIN-NICK PUT YOU UP TO THIS, RIGHT?"

Tears flow down Kissinger's cheeks. For the first time, I see the bags below his eyes, the dried rivers running across his cheeks. It's a face that has seen death.

"Pull the drigger," he whimpers.

Baldy approaches, smiling in a fatherly way, and slowly removes his glasses. Behind them are gamma rays.

Faces change, bodies change, but *eyes* are *eyes*.

A flash of shoe leather. Snap, crackle, pop.

I wake up on a bench in Grand Central Station with five hundred dollars taped to the palm of my hand. My jaw is the size of a grapefruit. I wander until my head clears, then go to Bernie's to contemplate transmissions from Mars.

Pork Fiction

THE STRAW HOUSE

Look, all I'm saying is thatched roofs, for fuel efficiency, consistently outperform gingerbread. The foliage traps heat in winter and cools you down in summer. In Bimini, you see this stuff everywhere.

Gimmie a break. This place looks like a dead Chia Pet. Man, this pig is living in a Mother Goosin' haystack.

Hey, he's a pig. Whaddaya expect? Aluminum siding? You ever eat pig?

Negativo. I don't do swine.

C'mon—bacon? You don't like bacon?

Imitation bacon bits, sometimes. Way I see it, a wolf lowers himself by eating hog. Me, I'm partial to poultry.

Hey, did he say there's three of them? You think we need shotguns?

C'mon, man. We're wolves. They're pigs. What're they gonna do? Whip us with their curly tails? By the way, you hear about Harry? Word has it Woodsman chopped off his head over that Red Riding Hood situation. They say he ate her gramma and was eyeballing her in the bedroom, but then this guy runs in, swinging his ax and screaming like Chicken frickin' Little. Whacked the brother's head clean off. Now, I ask you, is that right?

Way I heard it, the dude was camped in gramma's bed, wearing gramma's Playtex living girdle. I mean, a wolf ain't supposed to do that.

You saying it's OK to go Jayne Mansfield on a brother simply because he's between gramma's sheets, wearing gramma's unmentionables? That what you're saying?

Look, I'm saying I agree that Woodsman overreacted, but Harry should've known better. Eat your meal, but don't play with your food. That's all.

Interesting point. OK, it's time. Let's get in character.

Knock knock.

Little pig, little pig . . . THE PATH OF THE RIGHTEOUS MAN . . .

THE BRICK HOUSE

Piggy, are they coming after us?

Yeah, Pork Chop.

Will they get in?

No.

Thump.

What's that? In the living room. Oh, baby, I'm scared.

Wait here, Piglet. I'll be right back.

Pig peers around the corner and sees Wolf at the fireplace, beating on his smouldering tail. He empties a .45 into Wolf, splitting open his belly and causing blood to pour out onto the thick shag carpet. Wolf staggers and falls, writhing, into a cauldron of boiling water.

THE TWIG HOUSE

What happened back there was an act of God, you hear what I'm saying? That whole damn house just exploded, blew apart like cheap Kleenex. It's a miracle we're alive.

Hey, it was luck. That's all. Like you said, it was just a haystack, and this wood shanty looks just as cheap. Jesus, the pig didn't even bother to use nails. How do they live like that? Let's go get him.

No way. I'm quitting. First, it's that Red Riding Hood incident, then the straw hut, and now this— we're cruising Fairy Land with a dead pig in the backseat. I've had it. I ain't huffing these sticks. I'm outtahere.

C'mon, man, you can't quit. How you gonna live?

Way I see it, I'm gonna be a lone wolf. Gonna find me a flock of sheep guarded by some punk with a reputation for calling in false alarms, and I'm just gonna, you know, chill with the lambs.

You're full of it. No sheep's gonna trust you. Look at you. You're salivating now, just thinking about 'em. C'mon, man, you're a big bad wolf. This is your job. You can't just quit.

Done deal. Know what's wrong with this world? There's too many fairy frickin' godmothers flying around, granting wishes. Everybody expects to win at Lotto. Nobody wants to take responsibility. Well, that's what I'm doing.

You know, I used to recite the Brothers Grimm because I thought the tales offered clear distinctions between good and evil. The older I get, the more I figure those stories just tell about the weak and the strong. Life is a choice between the two. Yeah, I'm a big bad wolf. But I can change. What happened back there was a sign. I'm gonna heed it. From here on, I'm living happily evermothergoosinafter.

Steinbrenner in Love

||||||||||||||||||||||||||||||||||||||||||||||||||||||||||||||||||||||||||||||||||||||||||||||||||

Excerpts from King George III, *the newly discovered play penned by William Shakespeare.*

February.
ACT I, SCENE I. In a field. Thunder and lightning.

RIZZUTO: Single, double; bullpen trouble.

Owner burn and pitcher bubble.

Though great'st by far his minions be,

They're not great'st by far, enough, for he.

What huckl'berries these mortals be!

YOGI: 'Tis déjà vu—again, I see.

(Enter George, holding ball.)

GEORGE: O'er my hearth doth hang the bejeweled broom of series swept.

Yet the stone floor mocks surly 'neath a new season's dirt.

O, budget: Thou art paid to brutish beasts!

O Bernie! O Jeter! O Rivera! O'Neill!

And Good David Wells! The hurler burly! Paw
of south!

Thane of ale and team!

ALL: Maker of the perfect
game!

GEORGE: Ye hath restored the crown to its rightful
throne.

Alas, one soul whose yonder curveball breaks

Holds my heart in his split-fingered grip.

O, Roger Clemens, rocket of northern skies
domed.

No owner hath lesser need for thee, and yet:

This is the A.L. East, and Roger is the Cy Young.

RIZZUTO: Holy cow! His heart's imprison'd!

YOGI: To be, it is. To b'not, it isn't.

*ACT II, SCENE III. In the owner's box. Enter
Ghost.*

GEORGE: Angels and ministers of security, defend
me!

What botch of nature doth appear before me?

GHOST: I am the spirit of ye managers fired.

I bring news sure to screaming headlines capture.

To-night, the Jays tender Clemens to the bidder
high.

His breast shall be pin-striped before the cock
   crows.

But the ransom shall cut sharper than an agent's
   tooth:

To-night, David Wells shall from thy castle be
   snatched,

And ye shall be the robber.

GEORGE: Nay! That the heart of my rotation I would
   sell?

'Tis a trade rumor told by an idiot, signifying
   nothing.

True, Clemens in my coat could capture six-
   and-twenty.

But to peddle dear David; aye, there's the rub.

'Tis nobler in the mind to keep him.

GHOST: Owner, is not your summer of discontent
   foreseen?

Your staff shall wilt 'neath the gravity of in-
   nings hurled.

Put a pennant in thy purse.

Your Wells has drunk ten cups to-night,

And not the milk of human kindness.

Come May, he will be as full of quarrel and offense

As old Ripken's back.

Put a pennant in thy purse.

Clemens' hard heaves still bloody his receiver's
   leathered palm.
He painteth corners and maketh music of men's
   chins.
Lash Wells to a lesser pair and etch their travel
   tickets,
To-ronto, and To-ronto, and To-ronto.
Put a pennant in thy purse.
(Ghost exits.)

GEORGE: Wine of victory: Must thou always roil
   from rott'd fruit?
Torre, quickly! Screw your courage to the
   trading-place!

Opening Day.
ACT V, SCENE VIII. In a dugout.

RIZZUTO: The unkind'st cut doth poorly sells.

YOGI: All is not well that endeth Wells. . . .

GEORGE: O what a rouge and peasant owner I am!
   Betrayal: Thou art known to me as wife.
   (George points a dagger to his heart.)
   Good-bye, good team. Parting is such sweet sor-
   row.
   (Cashman enters.)

CASHMAN: My liege! Saint Louis whispers dangerous truths into my ear.

McGwire, the Ruthian knight, doth be for sale.

(George throws away the dagger.)

GEORGE: Hark, hark, the Mark!

Cashman, quickly! Send Tino Martinez to the
block.

Cut the deal!

CASHMAN: Et, Tino, boss?

GEORGE: A row of murderers I shall have. O what
teams may come!

RIZZUTO: Unb'lievable! What? A minute, wait!

L'mmie get this in, 'fore 'tis too late.

Get well, Ophelia, in Albany.

YOGI: 'Tis over now, 'cause ov'r it be.

Nineteen Ninety-four

It was a cold day in April, and the digital clocks were flashing thirteen. Winston Smith scanned his card at the door, nodded respectfully to the security camera outside No. 4, and began leafing through the letters that spilled from his mailbox. They came from celebrities hoping to save wildlife and from the chief executive officers of global corporations. "Dear W. Smith," one said. "Have you ever sent a fax from the beach? YOU WILL."

This rattled Winston. He feared beaches, where hot sands often concealed medical wastes. For a frightening moment, Winston wondered if he really wanted the freedom to watch five hundred TV channels or access the electronic-data super-highway from a laptop computer. To calm himself, Winston swallowed a Prozac, grabbed his precious remote box, and flicked on the telescreen. A woman with the piercing, all-knowing eyes of a TV reporter smiled at him. He knew her as Murphy.

"Trying to figure out which telephone company gives you the best deal?" Murphy said. "Only Sprint offers you The Most. It's like a billion-megabyte brain in your phone. It figures out who you call the most, then gives you a twenty percent discount on long-distance rates to that number. It's *that* simple."

Winston broke into a cold sweat. He'd heard of rebel phone companies but until now had never dreamed of joining one. Murphy vanished from the screen, replaced by a show devoted to the capture of criminals. But Winston still thought about Murphy.

"I will," he said finally, dialing the number she had projected. "I WILL!"

That night, Winston dreamed of making love to Murphy and saving 20 percent on long-distance rates.

He awoke next morning to the telescreen, where a large, bald man stood before a map of Oceana. "Here's what's happening in your world as we speak," the man said. Winston waited for instructions. The phone rang. A frantic voice shouted, "We want you back, W. Smith! WE WANT YOU BACK!"

This rattled Winston. He thought about nothing else while riding the train to the Ministry of Truth, where he worked in the Department of Conventional Wisdom. That morning, a programmer named O'Brien pulled Winston into a back room.

"We heard through e-mail that you're switching," O'Brien whispered. "Before you do, think about it. Think about what's important.

"I'm making a list, Smith," O'Brien continued. "It's my 'Friends and Family Circle' list. You could be on it. But in return, we need a list from you. We need to know whom we can count on. Join MCI, and you'll cut long-distance bills by twenty percent. Of course, certain restrictions apply. What do you say, comrade? Will you join?"

"I will," Winston said. "I WILL."

O'Brien's beeper sounded. The two men scurried to their workstations.

That night, as Winston entered No. 4, his phone was ringing. Before he could answer it, three intruders leaped from the shadows and pressed the Yellow Pages to Winston's mouth. His mind went blank.

Later, all he would remember were the words "Have a nice day."

He awoke lashed to a chair. At a console sat O'Brien.

"It was the Talk Police, Smith!" the programmer whimpered. "They reached out and touched me. They showed me . . . Reason Number 101."

"Dear God!" Winston said. He had heard of the more than eight hundred reasons not to leave AT&T. The mere thought of Reason 101 turned his bowels to water.

"Answer one question, and we'll release you!" O'Brien said. "With the other companies, how much do you save?"

"That's easy, O'Brien. I save up to twenty percent. It's that sim—AHHH."

A painful busy signal shot through Winston's body.

"Let me repeat my question, sir! How much do you *save?*"

"O'Brien, you know the answer! Up to twenty perce—AHHH!"

"YOU SAVE PENNIES, SMITH! DO YOU HEAR? PENNIES! FOR PENNIES, YOU GIVE UP *SERVICE,* SMITH. IT'S JUST AN-OTHER PART OF 'THE I PLAN.' YOU GIVE UP SERVICE—FOR PENNIES!"

"But O'Brien, you said—AHHHH—"

Months later, his resistance broken, Winston

shouted the answer O'Brien sought and came to recite the slogans of TrueVoice:

Clarity Is Peace.

Interruptions Are Slavery.

Caller ID Is Security.

After his release, Winston never again listened to
Murphy on his telescreen. He accepted without
question all the coming technologies. He never
went anywhere without his laptop. He had won the
struggle over himself. He loved Ma Bell and Big
Blue.

Captain's Log

||||||||||||||||||||||||||||||||||||||||||||||||||||||||||||||||||||||||||||||||||||||||||||||||||||||||||

Star date 5973.4: A strange, ancient morality has invaded the Enterprise, *turning my crew against me. I stand accused of sexual harassment, lewd behavior, and conduct unbecoming of an officer. No longer able to trust anyone, I have chosen to defend myself at the preliminary inquest that could decide my fate. . . .*

. . . And so, Mr. Scott, would you please tell the court exactly what Captain Kirk ordered you to do that night?

Aye, laddie. The captain, he had me lock the transporter onto the green lady's coordinates, and then—well—he told me to beam the clothes off of her.

And, did you?

Nay, laddie. I made up a story. I told him the dilithium crystals were cracked, and the ship, she just couldn't take it.

No further questions. Your honor, I move for the

immediate court-martial of James T. Kirk on the grounds that his repeated acts of sexual misconduct violate time-honored Star Fleet codes.

Sir, we've seen depositions from 134 female crew members and sixty-four alien species, all who swear they were propositioned by the captain. We learned how Kirk, using Romulan cloaking technology, made covert visits to the ladies' changing room. We know that the captain asked Dr. McCoy to treat his sexually transmitted space spores, and we heard from the ship's science officer, who characterized Kirk's behavior as—I'm quoting now—"highly illogical."

Your honor, the media have had a field day over the forced resignation of Lieutenant Uhura, due to charges that she and the captain pushed their alternative lifestyles on alternative life-forms. I submit that Uhura is the victim. The perpetrator is James T. Kirk, a modern-day Bill Clinton who has roamed this galaxy with his own prime directive: to seduce every female being that happens to engage his warped drive. I demand a verdict of guilty!

Thank you, Counselor Starr. Indeed, the evidence does seem overwhelming. Captain, have you anything to say?

I do, your honor. . . .

I am James T. Kirk, captain of the USS *Enterprise!* And I will not relinquish control of this ship! Scotty, Bones, Spock! Snap out of it! Remember last Thursday, when the *Enterprise* passed through that cloud of ionized estrogen particles? I was in my quarters with Yeoman Rand. I was straightening her uniform when I suddenly felt a backlash. I think that cloud was, in fact, a sentient being that has infiltrated our minds. This thing, whatever it is, turns men and women against each other!

WE . . . MUST . . . FIGHT . . . THIS . . . THING!

Your honor, are we so enslaved by this cloud that we have forgotten the traditions of military self-preservation? To kill this creature, we must do as officers have always done. We must close ranks! We must raise our shields!

Because let me remind you, gentlemen . . .

Nobody here is squeaky clean.

Spock, don't think I'm unaware of what you do during those mind melds. And Scotty, how many women have you invited down to engineering to examine your "antimatter pods"? Bones, didn't you once have some trouble with Tribbles? And your honor, didn't you divorce your first wife after finding out that, in fact, she was a shape-shifting man?

I OBJECT, YOUR HONOR! Kirk is trying to coer—

Pipe down, Starr! Objection overruled. The captain here has raised some interesting points. . . .

Captain's Log Supplemental: After long negotiations, I have accepted an honorable discharge, with full compensation and the sealing of all court records. I have begun work on my book and also plan to do some consulting for Star Fleet. Tomorrow, I set a course for my new five-year mission—on the pleasure planet, Raisa. Indeed, I plan to boldly go where no man has gone before.

Doctor Dosomething

> *If I could talk to the animals.*
> —*Doctor Dolittle,* children's classic, now out on video

> *We have this time on the air to focus on how to*
> *be not just human animals but moral animals.*
> —Doctor Laura, radio's most popular therapist

Hello, Simba, king of beasts, welcome to the Dr. Laura Dolittle Show. What's on your mind?

Doctor, it's my son. First, he shaves his mane. Then he says he don't wanna be king. Last night at the table, he tells me he won't eat meat. Says it's all wrong, says he won't eat anything with a face. Now I hear he's dating an antelope. We're carnivores, for Pete's sake! What the hell is it with these kids?

It's bad parenting, Simba. That's the problem. Tell me, what quality time do you spend with your son?

We used to do a lot of things together. When he

was young, on weekends, we'd go in and eat a whole village. Now, he says that's cruel. He's even threatening to have himself declawed.

Simba, how do you expect to control the jungle when you can't even control your own child? When he first stepped out of line, did you discipline him? Like many of your generation, you've given your kid too much freedom. Now you've got to rein him in.

Thanks, Laura. You're right. When he gets home from the fur protest, he's gonna get it.

Hello, Buster Bulldog in Michigan. Speak.

Hi, Laura. Lately, when my master's out, I've been getting up on the couch. I know I'm not supposed to, but I just sort of do it. And I'm wondering, does that make me a bad dog?

Why the couch, Buster?

Oh, wow. It was always this way. Going up there, it's—well—empowering.

Are you on the couch now?

No. Well . . . yeah.

Did you ever read my book, *Ten Things Dogs Do to Mess Up the Furniture*?

Yeah. Well, actually, no. I'm not good with books. I chew them.

Does your master know about the couch?

I think he suspects. I try not to shed or stain the upholstery, but there's only so much you can do.

Buster, how long have you been pulling these stunts to get attention?

Look, Laura, this isn't my fault. He forced me into this. He doesn't care anymore. Ever since I got fixed, he doesn't even want to pet me.

Buster, I hear this all the time: "My master doesn't understand me. I want something more. So it's OK to go up on the couch; *he's* the one who left me alone. It's OK to drink out of the toilet; *he* left the seat up. I've got *me* to think about—and by the way, what's for supper?" It's always the same. "Feed *me,* pet *me,* walk *me.*" Well, let me tell you: It's time for you to grow up and learn some new tricks, Buster. It's time for you to take responsibility—time for you to *heel.*

You're right, Laura. Thanks.

One more thing: GET OFF THE COUCH, NOW! Hello, Guppie Goldfish from Newark, what's on your mind?

Oh, doctor . . . what should I do? I JUST ATE MY BABIES!

Guppie, listen to me: This is bad. I don't care if you couldn't afford decent child care. For a mom, you are an absolute disgrace. I have said this a thousand times, but let me say it again: I am totally opposed to the eating of one's young. It is a tragedy. It is immoral. It is fattening. And it has got to stop. Next caller. Marge, what's up?

Laura, I can't take it anymore. My husband is a sloth!

Patriot Games

With a $350 million stadium, guaranteed luxury-seat revenues, and a $1 billion riverfront development, the city of Hartford, Connecticut, last year almost lured the National Football League's New England Patriots to town. "We want to redefine Hartford's place on the map," Connecticut governor John Rowland said. "We want to be more than a mile marker between Boston and New York."

The deal eventually fell through. But what exactly did Hartford have in mind?

Graceland, the Memphis-based home to the late Elvis Presley, will move to Hartford, Connecticut, beginning in 2002, officials announced today.

Graceland executives, speaking from Hartford, stressed that Elvis will always call Memphis his home, but he is dead, and with old celebrities joining him every day he needed to "find a new place to dwell" to compete with larger-market shrines. The ownership had threatened to leave since April, after Tennessee voters rejected a proposed $400 million Hyatt Regency Heartbreak Hotel Convention Center.

To get Graceland, Hartford agrees to build the seventy-thousand-seat mausoleum/theme park, "Graceworld," which will be financed through the sale of luxury double-wides and a 5 percent surcharge on velvet portraits.

"Elvis has left the state!" Connecticut governor John Rowland said. "Viva Hartford!"

Grand Canyon officials today announced plans to move the popular U.S. park to Hartford, Connecticut, where it will coanchor a $30 billion downtown redevelopment, beginning in fiscal year 2003.

Though anticipated, the news sent political and geological shock waves across the western states, crushing a last-ditch campaign to save the franchise. But after failing last May to renegotiate its two-million-year lease with Arizona, the canyon began shopping itself to larger media markets. Ever since, Arizona public officials have sought a suitable replacement, rumored to be Knott's Berry Farm.

The new seven-hundred-thousand-seat Grand Hartford Canyon will feature a retractable dome, artificial turf, IMAX theater, shopping mall, golf course, and Trump Palace Casino. The thirty-year agreement calls for Hartford to guarantee $200 million annually from canyon wall advertising.

"The future looks grand!" Governor John Rowland said. "We want to be the biggest hole between Boston and Los Angeles!"

Vatican officials confirmed today that the pope has signed a memorandum of intent to move his world headquarters to Hartford, Connecticut, after the current lease expires on December 25, 2004.

The proposed Hartford Vatican will include a $900 million domed cathedral/parking garage and holy water park, capping the city's two-thousand-year quest to capture a major religion. Last May, attempts to lure the Wailing Wall fell through, after Jerusalem voters approved construction of a six-million-seat prayer/retail/residential center called "HolyLand."

To lure the pope, the city and state will guarantee $270 million in annual donations, to be raised through corporate sponsorships, bake sales, bingo, and reinvigorated Friday fish fries.

"Hartford has been blessed!" Governor John Rowland confessed. "We want to be the Greatest Story Ever Told!"

. . .

Afterlife officials today said the Netherworld of Hell will move to Hartford, Connecticut, beginning in 2007.

The announcement, which would leave Hell without a franchise for the first time in history, unleashed a chorus of anguished screams from its doomed minions, yet furnace ownership remained unrepentant. Faced with rampant overcrowding and the skyrocketing costs of tempting free-agent souls, underworld officials last April proposed construction of an eight-trillion-seat fiery pit, but the measure was cast out. A Satanic spokesman vowed to fill the void with a replacement, rumored to be Knott's Berry Farm.

To raise Hell, the city and state promised to build a $2 billion domed inferno, called Hellford, which will include a fiery theme park, lava pits with air-conditioned luxury boxes, Museum of the Damned Hall of Fame, and a Planet Hollywood. The project will be financed through the sale of Connecticut souls for the next three hundred years.

"When people think of Hell, they're going to think of Hartford!" Governor John Rowland said. "We must be in heaven!"

Dressing for Oppress

IIIIIIIIIIIIIIIIIIIIIIIIIIIIIIIIIIIIIIIIIIIIIIIIIIIIIIIIIIIIIIIIIIIIIIIIIIIIIIIIIIIIIIIIIIIIIIIIIIIII

Next on CNN: In today's troubled world of corporate downsizing and social uncertainty, the hottest trend in fashion is looking the loser! Elsa Klensch views a new collection for white males who are celebrating their sexual and political oppression!

Hello from Utica! I'm Elsa Klensch with a special edition of *Style!* We're here today to glimpse the latest designs from Mr. Benny, whose visionary theme, "Dress for Oppression," promises to let our Caucasian cogs in the corporate carousel view themselves as they really are: the true victims!

Joining me for this extraordinary event is my fashion cohost, my color man, Mr. John Madden.

ELSA, THEY WERE TALKING ABOUT BENNY. THEY WERE SAYING HE'S GETTING OLD, THAT HE'S COLOR-BLIND, THAT THE HANDS CAN'T DO THE STITCHING ANYMORE. BUT I'VE BEEN GOING TO BENNY'S BIG-AND-TALL-MAN

SHOP FOR YEARS, AND I CAN TELL YOU THIS GUY'S GOT A LOT OF CLOTHES LEFT IN HIM. AND IT'S GOOD TO SEE THE TIMES FINALLY CATCHING UP, BECAUSE WHEN THEY TALK ABOUT WHITE GUYS LOOKING DEPRESSED, BELIEVE ME, THEY TALK ABOUT BENNY.

John, here's our first model. It's Cooter, taking a well-deserved break from the keyboard to stand in the rain and smoke a cigarette. He wears a phone book–yellow headset made by Tandy and, over his free ear, a matching Mongol No. 2 pencil. Cooter's tan trousers ride a quarter inch above his white tube socks, ventilating the midcalf, and his tie reeks of birthday gift. The shirt pocket is logoed with a dollop of exploded-pen ink, and note the sleeves, John. They're rolled up, for an accessory that screams, "Pity me": Velcro-fastened, ergonomic wrist supports!

I WAS TALKING TO COOTER BEFORE THE SHOW, ELSA, AND HE'S MODELING HURT. IT'S THAT CARPAL-TUNNEL THING THAT YOU GET IN YOUR HANDS. BUT COOTER'S THE TYPE OF MODEL WHO—JUST HIS PRESENCE OUT THERE

HELPS THIS COLLECTION. CHECK OUT THE REPLAY: HE MAKES A HECK OF A STROLL... TAKES OUT HIS LIGHTER ... DOESN'T LIGHT ... DOESN'T LIGHT ... DOESN'T LIGHT ... BOOM! ... LIGHTS! I MEAN, WHEN YOU SEE A GUY WEARING THOSE WRIST PADS, YOU KNOW THAT GUY IS OPPRESSED. AND YOU GOTTA HAND IT TO COOTER. HE'S POSING IN PAIN. HE'S NOT A HUNDRED PERCENT. A LOT OF GUYS WOULDN'T BE OUT THERE RIGHT NOW, BUT IN A BIG SHOW NO ONE WANTS COOTER IN THERE MORE THAN COOTER.

Hold everything, John. Here comes Herb, mixing business with pleasure—and gin with tonic! He's off to the golf course with his district manager and a prospective customer. Herb wears a super-nova-purple fedora, traffic light–green pants, white golf shoes, and a tequila sunset–orange polo shirt that treats us to an inch of furry midriff. And by the way, John, do you know why Herb golfs with two pairs of pants?

It's in case he gets a *hole* in *one!*

THIS GOLF GAME IS NINETY-FIVE

PERCENT MENTAL, ELSA, SO YOU NEED MENTAL CLOTHES. THE KEY HERE IS THE COLORS, BECAUSE YOU DEFINITELY CAN SEE THESE GUYS COMING. YOU REALLY GOTTA LOOK HARD TO FIND COLORS LIKE THAT, AND BENNY HAS DONE A HECK OF A JOB HERE. I DON'T KNOW WHERE HE GOT THESE COLORS. THERE MUST'VE BEEN A SALE SOME-PLACE. HE MUST'VE FOUND SOME HIGHWAY-SIGN PAINT DOWN IN HIS BASEMENT. I MEAN, THESE ARE THE KIND OF COLORS YOU WEAR FOR HUNT-ING, SO THE OTHER GUY DOESN'T SHOOT YOU. YOU WEAR THESE COLORS, AND PEOPLE WILL THINK YOU'RE OP-PRESSED. I GUARANTEE YOU THAT.

Stand back, John, and paint it black! Here comes Brian, our classic rocker, who plans to get some "satisfaction" at the Rolling Stones tribute show! Brian's faux ponytail dangles into his tie-dyed T-shirt, and his torn jeans are kept in place by both a belt and suspenders. Sandals enclose his dark socks—one black, one navy—and Brian's fanny pack holds the essentials: earplugs, binoculars, and "stash." And that aroma creeping our way, John, is the new fragrance by Calvin Klein, *Oppression,* a ruddy mix of Desenex and Absorbine Jr.

YOU KNOW BENNY'S INTO IT WHEN HE'S MIXING UP THE SMELLS. BUT THE KEY HERE, I THINK, IS THE BELT-SUSPENDERS COMBO. IN THIS LEAGUE, YOU GOTTA HAVE BACKUPS. I MEAN, WHAT IF THE SUSPENDERS GO? THEN YOUR PANTS WOULD BE DOWN AT YOUR ANKLES! CAN'T STRESS IT ENOUGH. YOU GOTTA HAVE BACKUPS.

Look, John! Here's Ted, kissing his wife good-bye, as he heads off for a grueling weekend business trip. His gray flannel suit with white shirt and power tie, coupled with his briefcase and black loafers, illustrate Ted's "nose to the grindstone" approach to the job. Nevertheless, all work and no play makes Ted a dull boy. So with one strategic pull on the zipper (the suit reverses), here's *Teddy*— in full-body leather bondage gear, with matching love-slave collar! John? John?

And now for a change of pace. Here comes Ed, hiking merrily to his secret paramilitary convention! Whether you're a soldier of fortune or an unfortunate soldier, this ensemble will have the fashion militia shouting, "A-ten-chun!" Ed's traditional camouflage suit, courtesy of Benny's Army-Navy Store, opens to reveal a black screaming-skull T-shirt. Atop his khaki bandanna rests a pair of low-light goggles, and slung over Ed's shoulder is a fully loaded M-16. And, John, check out Benny's ironic note here: jackboots!

TO ME, THIS MILITIA THING IS WHAT IT'S ALL ABOUT. IF BENNY IS GOING TO CREATE STYLES, IF HE IS GOING TO SELL CLOTHES, IF HE IS GOING TO SHOW THE ALIENATION OF WHITE MALES, HE NEEDS THESE GUYS. THE GUN NUTS HAVE GOT TO TAKE CONTROL OF THE BALL GAME. BECAUSE THESE ARE THE REAL CRAZIES. THEY REALLY THINK THEY'RE OPPRESSED—THEY FIGURE EVERYBODY'S OUT TO GET THEM. YOU HEAR THE OTHERS' NAMES CALLED ALL THE TIME—YOUR OLLIE NORTHS, YOUR G. GORDON LIDDYS, YOUR RUSH LIMBAUGHS—BUT THEY'VE GOTTEN SOFT. THESE MILITIA TYPES, THEY DON'T TALK, THEY DON'T VOTE, THEY DON'T PAY TAXES, THEY JUST STARE AT YOU. SO

IF THERE'S GOING TO BE PERSECUTION OF WHITE MALES, THESE ARE THE GUYS WHO'LL MAKE IT HAPPEN!

Apparently, we're out of time. For *Style,* I'm Elsa Klensch reminding everyone: You're the victim, so dress like one!

Story Days

Songs by Phil Collins boosted this summer's hit animated motion picture Tarzan. *Is this the future of rock?*

This summer, treat your family to a musical spectacular of mystery and wonder, a story that has delighted working men and women for ages! Walt Disney Motion Pictures presents the magical tale of a young sprout from Jersey who was born to climb. . . .

> *In the deep dark woods or out on the street*
> *Of a runaway American gloom,*
> *At night we climb extensions of flora*
> *From suicide legumes. . . .*

Yes, the beanstalk's jammed with broken heroes when the fantasy of Walt Disney and the morality of Bruce Springsteen team up to bring you *Beanstreets!* You'll travel back to a bygone era and meet

Jack, the tough-talking-but-lovable Vietnam vet who gets laid off at the refinery and must sell his beloved 1972 Dodge Dart. . . .

> *The car door slams,*
> *Mary's trunk waves.*
> *Like a Buick she sputters across the lot,*
> *As her radiator sprays. . . .*

This summer, case the promised land with Jack, his girlfriend Candy, and a cast of characters only Disney and the Boss could create. You'll meet the Magic Rat, Crazy Janey, Jack the Rabbit and Weak Knees Willie, Sloppy Sue and Big Bones Billy. They'll be coming up for air! Because when Jack needs $2,500 to cover child-support payments and debts no honest man can pay, he heads to the board-walk to see the mysterious Madam Marie. . . .

> *Show a little faith!*
> *There's magic in the beans,*
> *It ain't a dollar, but hey,*
> *They're all green. . . .*

It's *Beanstreets!* the classic tale mixed with classic rock! And after Jack gets into an argument with his

dad, who's out on disability with the gout, his ex-
wife Sandy tosses the beans into the parking lot of
an abandoned factory—and something incredible
takes root. . . .

Thrown down in a dead man's town,
The first sprouts, they took
Before they hit the ground. . . .
Grown in the U.S.A. . . .

Featuring the voices of Matt Damon as Jack,
Heather Graham as Rosie the talking harp, Clarence Clemons as the Big Man, and Howie Mandell
as Tramp, the incredible goose that lays golden
eggs. . . .

Jackie, let me in, I wanna be your hen,
I wanna buy you tea and crumpets.
Just check my eggs with the Franklin Mint
And write your checks off my omelettes. . . .

You'll visit Gigantic City, that world above the
clouds, where everything that dies someday comes
back. But when Jack meets the Corporate Giant, it's
a death trap, it's a suicide rap. . . .

And the goslings down here
Don't lay nothin' at all,
They just honk back
And let it all be. . . .

Don't waste your summer prayin' in vain! Because the fireworks are hailin' over *Beanstreets!*—coming to theaters on the edges of towns everywhere. And in time for Christmas 2000, Bob Dylan *is* Alexander Graham Bell. . . .

But I would not feel so all alone,
EVERYBODY MUST GET PHONED!

The Electric Kool-Aid Antacid Test

Ken Kesey's current bus tour, reliving his Merry Pranksters' cross-country trip in 1964, could inspire an update from Tom Wolfe. . . .

"Next exit, pull over?" (O, the pain—)
"BUT I WOULD NOT . . . FEEL SO ALL ALONE . . ."
"Next exit, please." (O, the freakin' pain!)
"EVERYBODY! . . . MUST! . . . GET! . . . STONED!"
"C'mon, guys! Next exit, PULL OVER!"
Hey, Tummytuck, chill. I am sitting with Tummytuck, a literary agent with a three-day goatee and the cultured whine of an Ivy League president, which is designed to say: I've grown tired of this ride, this singing, and suggest we stop somewhere for a strawberry-blond lager and some wood-fired pizza. We're doing seventy-five in a sixty-five-mile zone, racing to make Ann Arbor in time for Kesey

to do the Action News Live Eye at Six, then the book signing at Borders. For Tummytuck, the tight schedule is a serious bummer, because four mocha lattes and the bouncing of the bus have launched a two-pronged assault on his swollen prostate, and he needs a freaking rest room so badly he can taste it.

"Hold on until Michigan!" Carpal-Tunnel Girl howls from the back, flashing a Day-Glo, it's-a-manly-deodorant-but-I-like-it-too smile, gorked on ginseng and a sugar cube laced with Melatonin, which might help her survive this all-you-can-eat bellyache of a bad trip. During the Chinese fire drill in Chicago, she slammed her shin into Further's back bumper, and, YEOW, it still hurts to stand. The bus's psychedelic pattern is giving her a migraine, not to mention her son, Brandon, who just called from Stanford to say he totaled the Range Rover. She accepts a hit from the Pepto-Bismol bottle being passed. "JUST KEEP GOING!"

Too late. Triple Bypass jerks the steering wheel, EAUGH, careening the bus, EAUUGH, onto the off-ramp, EAUUUUUGH, and into the parking lot of an A.M.–P.M. minimart, silencing the songs, halting the bridge game, and rousing nappers from their happy dreams. Soon, the Pranksters hobble out, stretching sciatica, lighting cigarettes, sucking in guts, buttoning pants, resetting hairpieces, and blinking fresh droplets of Visine, as a Dylan CD wails, "Ah, but I was so much older then, I'm younger than that now."

"Oh, wow, man!" Kidney Stone shouts, discovering the nose-ringed, shaven-headed cash-register attendant. "Look, everybody, it's Pirate Boy!"

"No, it's Nosemetal Q. Youngfellow!" Miracle Ear proclaims, waving his cigar. "Roadside retailer extraordinaire!"

"I don't see fat-free Ben & Jerry's," Trophy Wife asks, jabbing the counter with a Visa card. "Got any fat-free Ben & Jerry's? Fat-free Ben & Jerry's!"

"FAT-FREE BEN & JERRY'S!! FAT-FREE BEN & JERRY'S!!"

"HEY, SHUDDUP, PEOPLE! I'M TALKING TO CLEVELAND," 401(k) yells, cradling a cell phone to his ear. "Listen, Phil, we still got 543 T-shirts in stock, and we're cutting a big-time loss on the tote bags. I told you, man, this logo sucks. Nobody listened. I said we should take the Nike deal, but nobody listened, and now we're screwed, because this logo sucks!

"Hey, Ringbeak," 401(k) says to the clerk, showing off his shirt. "Would you wear this piece of crap?"

When the cashier looks confused, 401(k) waves him off and offers a paternal smile.

"Aw, forget it, kid. Don't let us crazy hippie freaks blow your mind. Just do your own thing. If you're into workin' here on Maggie's farm, that's cool. But make your own kind of music. Stand up for what you believe in. And don't never let no Doo-Dah man tell you otherwise!

"WHAT THE—?" He jerks to the phone. "WHADDAYA MEAN THEY'RE NOT THERE YET! You tell them kids to get their stoned-out asses to that bookstore by six, or we're callin' the cops! You hear me? What's with these kids today? Like I said, it's six o'clock at the TV station, six-thirty at the bookstore, eight at the hotel. Christ, I don't care what they told you! THE TIMES, THEY ARE NOT CHANGIN'!"

Raze the Titanic

Today in Hollywood history: March 23, 1998.
Beneath the joy of these Oscar ceremonies
lurks a terrifying dilemma: The most successful
movie of the year—perhaps of all time—
cannot birth a sequel. Right?

First off, I truly love you guys for having me here because I know you're busy, what with the speeches and humanitarian stuff, so I'll try to pitch this in less than the usual three minutes.

We begin with a submarine, cruising the North Atlantic. But it's not one of ours. It's a German U-boat. Suddenly, the commander's eyes bulge. He yells something in German. The subtitle: "ICE-BERG, DEAD AHEAD!" The sub turns, barely avoids the ice, but scrapes off a piece, exposing—a human hand!

Bang! We roll the credits. "Kate Winslet . . . Billy

Zane . . . George Clooney in . . . TITANIC II: JACK RESURRECTION!"

Flash to Germany 1936. A Nazi scientist, Dr. Klauss Von Schlumberg, examines the chunk of ice. Using a top-secret thawing process, stolen from an American named Clarence Birdseye, he brings Jack back to life!

Now here's the beauty of this: We don't need Leonardo DiCaprio. You sit eighty-six years in an ice cube, and it rearranges your face. In this case, Jack comes out as George Clooney. Or, if necessary, somebody cheap.

Anyway, Jack wakes up confused. He doesn't know about the Nazis. He thinks he's in Schenectady. When the Germans realize there's no current record of Jack's existence, they do what you'd expect: They train him to become the ultimate killing machine. Then they send him to America on a mission via—get this—the *Hindenburg!*

We'll build an exact duplicate of the blimp, right down to the sign: Goodyear! (That's a joke, guys.) Anyway, Jack rides in steerage, while the filthy-rich human trash in first class hang out in a ballroom, up on top.

Onboard, Jack spots Rose, his old *Titanic* sweetheart. She's trying to kill herself by breathing helium. Rose is bummed, because her mom hooked her up to marry a young Adolf Hitler. Of course, Rose doesn't love him. He's Hitler, for God's sake! But if Rose doesn't marry the guy, her mom will have to get a job.

Rose doesn't recognize Jack, because—hey—he's George Clooney. Jack talks her out of suicide by breathing helium and doing funny elf impersonations. But Hitler doesn't laugh. He yanks her away, and they walk the deck, where Hitler notes with pride that there are parachutes only for first-class passengers.

But somebody else is watching: Rose's former fiancé, Caledon Hockley. He's here to sell the Nazis something they desperately want: The Ark of the Covenant! Because, as everybody knows, an army that carries the Ark cannot be defeated!

Anyway, Hockley gets Jack arrested. They tie Jack up in the main control room, next to a panel of critical instruments. He manages to draw a sketch of Rose and slip it out the window, where she finds it and realizes that George Clooney is Jack.

Bang. We hit the flashback sequences, play the Celine Dion song.

Rose sets Jack free. But Hitler, being Hitler, tries to steal the Ark. Hockley goes nuts—did I mention he's on drugs?—and shoots the control panel, causing the *Hindenburg* to burst into flames.

Everyone has only two hours before the ship goes down. Hitler gets away in a makeshift plane. Hockley tears the parachute from a baby's arms and escapes. Jack and Rose run from flaming deck to flaming deck, until they reach the top of the blimp. They have one 'chute. Holding each other, they jump.

But the 'chute can't support two people. Falling, Jack tells Rose to go forth and prosper, to fight the Nazis, and to push for sexual equality while keeping her womanhood. Then he lets go and disappears into the clouds.

Last scene. Safe on the ground, Rose clutches Jack's sketch and books passage to her new home: Krakatoa, east of Java!

Well, questions? Sure, I can script it by Wednesday!

Sing Sing Danny Rose

Sure, he's crazy, mad as a hatter. What difference does it make? You know, a long time ago, being crazy meant something. Nowadays, everybody's crazy.
—Charles Manson, answering Diane Sawyer's question, "Is Charles Manson crazy?"

. . . And it's ba-boom! I've done all my best material, my biggest gag, my sharpest bit, and still no response. The guy's lying there like an oil painting, and *I'm* the one who's dying, and I'm thinking to myself, "Charlie, this killing stuff always worked in the past. Have I still got it?" Hey, you guys ever pull a Rasputin? They are absolute downers, am I right?

I hear you talking, Charlie, and I can really relate, but I gotta tell you, and I mean no disrespect here, but the diehard is a rarity nowhere else but in L.A. Back in those days—and I saw this man in L.A., and I swear to you guys, this man *killed* in

L.A., Charlie, you *murdered* them out there—and I'm not knocking the people in L.A., I love the crowds, I love the stars, but L.A. is not N.Y.C., do you hear what I'm saying? I'm just saying that Jimmy B. would never—

Breslin again! Give us a break with the Breslin thing, OK, Berkowitz? None of you guys know Midwest. I'm talking Chicago now, my old stomping grounds, where you find the toughest people anywhere.

Charlie, David, I agree with Mr. Gacy, because when I was back in Milwaukee—

What? YOU? SHUT UP, DAHMER, SHUT UP! Don't you ever interrupt, and don't you *ever* call this man "Charlie"! It is *Mister Manson* to you. Listen, you had one shtick: killing people and eating them. That's it. You ate 'em. That's all. So, you got on *Inside Edition*? So what? You're still a punk. This man here had *everything*. He had demon worship. He had a cult. You? You got nothing.

Go easy on the kid, Gace. *Hey, guard, you got fresh cream cheese for these bagels?* You know, kid, I was doing mental when you were in diapers. I was doing that wah-wah nutso act when you were a peanut in a shell. And people respect me for that. They know when they hear the name Charlie Manson, they're going to get top-shelf crazy. Like with Diane. She's a sweet kid. She comes to me, and she *knows* who does wacko. Swastika on the forehead? Zodiac didn't do that. Hillside didn't do that. *I* did that, and I was first. Diane appreciates this, so I help her out, toss her a few crumbs. In this business, a little respect goes a long way. Berky, am I right?

Damn right! So don't open your punk mouth here, Dahmer, because you are in the presence of more talent than you'll ever have. And don't give me that *Entertainment Tonight* spotlight sneer either. Just shut up and eat. You serial kids don't realize how good you have it today because of this man. I mean, when I was on top, I still remember Jimmy B.—

Here we go with the Breslin again. . . .

. . . Listen: People lined up to see *me,* but even to Jimmy B., this man here, Charlie, he was Chairman of the Board. You may be hot now, Dahmer, but let's see you in twenty years.

Kid, if I were you I'd listen, because Berky and the Clown were working the clubs long before you ever picked up a fork. You too, Chapman. We don't even want to hear from you. What did *you* do? *One?* One is lint! One is a night! You do not deserve to ever have Diane visit you! You are not worthy of

such a lady! You should get used to Geraldo, because that's where you'll always be. Yeah, it's been
more than twenty years, but I still got it. Every time
I'm up for parole, I'm front-page news. You Generation X'ers? Your type is a dime a dozen. You'll be
replaced. Me? I broke ground. I'm here to stay.
Gace, am I right?

Amen, Charlie, amen.

Guys, I'd love to stick and kibitz, but I'm doing a
project with Fox. I got meetings all day. *Hey, war-
den, check!* This one's on me.

Away from It All

||||||||||||||||||||||||||||||||||||||||||||||||||||||||||||||||||||||||||||||||||||||||||||||||||||||||

Bub and Satey thank you for renting on scenic Wrickey Lake. Please note these cabin rules and recommendations:

1. The locked basement is for storage only. Please stay out of this area.

2. The Vanderpools, who live on nearby Wrichard Bay, will remove your trash and recyclables, at no charge, nightly. Just leave unwanted items outside your cabin. (Note: Be sure to bring all wanted items inside.)

3. If, while hiking, you meet a group of stray dogs, remember that they generally are more afraid of you than you are of them. Simply toss aside whatever food you're carrying, then move slowly away. DO NOT RUN!

4. Please show respect for the flag that flies over the Vanderpool family compound. This signifies the Republic of Vanderpool, a sovereign nation sep-

arate from the United States since 1973. Trespassers could face interrogation or possible incarceration.

5. For day trips, we suggest nearby Potterfield (twenty-eight miles south on Route 182), home to the Exit 47 Truck Stop, which offers a $5.95 All-U-Can-Eat Grand Seafood Buffet, Tuesday through Friday. (Best to go before Friday.) Further south is Mr. Wiggly's Sausage Barn, where families can tour "the magic of meat from hoof to bun." Free samples. Also, don't forget Happy Land Park, featuring Big Rickety, the world's oldest and fastest wooden roller coaster, and Ultimate Pee Wee Fighting every Friday, the winner receiving a fifty-dollar savings bond. (If planning to enter, don't forget child's birth certificate!)

6. At night, you may have dreams about the basement or at times feel an overwhelming compulsion to see what's down there. Please, do not go in the basement.

7. Because of the high-intensity lines from Rainbow Valley Nuclear Units 1 and 2, radios, flashlights, and other electrical equipment may turn on and off spontaneously. (No pacemakers, please.) Also, inside the cabin, you may occasionally experience minor electric shocks. MAKE SURE YOU

ARE COMPLETELY DRY BEFORE USING ANY APPLIANCE!

8. You might hear shouts or explosions along Vanderpool Road between the hours of 11 P.M. and 4 A.M. These are routine field maneuvers conducted by General Vanderpool and his troops. If such noises occur, merely turn off all lights and remain inside your cabin.

9. Prolonged contact with lake water may irritate the skin. If problems occur, the Potterfield Burn Center (twenty-nine miles south on Route 182) is open twenty-four hours a day.

10. For religious services, you are invited to the Temple of Universal Truth, whose members are characterized by their shaven heads and black turtlenecks. Or visit their webpage. Some of the acolytes may be a bit persistent about inviting you to join them on a journey. We recommend against it, unless you plan an extended stay.

11. Don't be surprised if your family hears Girdie, the legendary monster that haunts Vanderpool Woods. The creature's fearsome roar could shake the cabin at about 5:18 each morning, as Girdie rumbles down the tracks in her daily migration.

12. Now and then, federal law-enforcement officials may institute a blockade around the Vanderpool Republic. If such a policy is enacted, ask the highest-ranking U.S. officer for a pass allowing your family access to and from the cabin. Upon request, Kevlar vests will be provided.

13. During your stay, you may have the pleasure of meeting "the Professor," who lives in the woods not far from your cabin. He is harmless, though it's best not to offend him by flaunting electronic devices. If you're heading to town, the Professor may ask you to mail a package for him. You'll be amazed at the folks with whom our favorite hermit corresponds.

14. As the cabin continues to settle, the creaks and groans of aging woodwork at times may sound almost as if someone is in the basement, begging to be freed. For your own well-being and your family's safety, please stay out of the basement.

The Six Degrees of Chuck Berry

With a grateful nod to Thomas Meehan

Hi, everybody! I'm Kathie Lee Gifford, and welcome to the Bankthemoney.com Music Excellence Awards. With cohost David Lee Roth, we'll meet some of the biggest names in the recording industry. Right, David Lee?

Totally, Kathie Lee! And here they come: Hollywood's Tommy Lee Jones, escorting singer Rickie Lee Jones, followed by bluesman John Lee Hooker, the legendary Jerry Lee Lewis, and rocker Tommy Lee. Hey, do you folks all know each other? No? Let me do introductions. . . .

Tommy Lee, John Lee. John Lee, Jerry Lee. Jerry Lee, Tommy Lee. Tommy Lee, Rickie Lee. Rickie Lee, John Lee. John Lee, Tommy Lee. Jerry Lee, Tommy Lee. Tommy Lee, Tommy Lee. Kathie Lee?

Thanks, David Lee. More artists are arriving, led by my own personal favorites, Boy George and Kid Rock. Hey, do you folks all know each other? No?

Boy, Kid. Mr. Rock, Jewel. Jewel, Cool. L.L., B.B. Mr. King, Mr. Hill. Dru, Lou. Mr. Bega, Ms. Vega. Suzanne, Celine. Ms. Dion, Mr. Zevon. Warren, Waylon. Mr. Jennings, Mr. Jagger. Mick, Nick. Mr. Lowe, Ms. Loeb. Lisa, Tina. Ms. Turner, Ms. Tucker. Tanya, Enya. Enya, Shania. Shania, Mariah. Mariah, Wynonna. Wynonna, Fiona. Ms. Apple, Mr. Berry. Chuck Berry, Buckcherry!

That's no little feat, Kathie Lee, but Buckcherry's a band! And more bands are arriving. Hey, do you folks all know each other? No?

Garbage, Biohazard. Biohazard, Anthrax. Anthrax, Megadeth. Megadeth, Genesis. Genesis, Live. Live, Offspring. Offspring, 10,000 Maniacs. Maniacs, Dummies. Crash Test Dummies, Goo Goo Dolls. Goo Goos, Go-Gos. Go-Gos, Toto. Toto, Kansas. Kansas, Alabama. Alabama, Bananarama. Bananarama, Chumbawumba. Chumbawumba, Eminem. Eminem, R.E.M. R.E.M., U2. U2, B-52s. B-52s, War. War, Bush. Bush, Presidents of the United States of America. Presidents, Barenaked Ladies. Barenaked Ladies, Squeeze. Squeeze, Sponge. Sponge, Cake. Cake, Cranberries. Cranberries, Buckcherry. Buckcherry, Chuck Berry!

Him again? Oh well, it's a crowded house, David Lee! And more artists are arriving, led by my own personal favorite, Ozzy Osbourne. Hey, do you folks all know each other? No?

Ozzy, Mr. Nelson. Willie, Billy. Mr. Bragg, Ms. Crow. Sheryl, Cher. Cher, Bono. Mr. Bono, Ms. Ono. Yoko, Coolio. Coolio, Julio. Mr. Iglesias, Ms. Imbruglia. Natalie, Natalie. Ms. Merchant, Mr. Cash. Johnny, Yanni. Yanni, Danny. Mr. Elfman, Mr. Ant. Adam Ant, Flea. Flea, Mr. Doggy Dogg. Snoop Doggy, Puff Daddy. Mr. Daddy, Mr. Pop. Iggy Pop, Brandy. Brandy, Mr. Berry. Chuck Berry, Buckcherry!

Them again? Oh well, they got lost in the traffic, no doubt. But more bands are arriving, Kathie Lee. Hey, do you folks all know each other? No?

Backstreet Boys, Indigo Girls. Indigo Girls, Dixie Chicks. Chicks, Styx. Styx, Stones. Rolling Stones, Jesus Jones. Jesus, Judas Priest. Judas, Godsmack. Godsmack, Smash Mouth. Smash Mouth, Kiss. Kiss, Yes. Yes, Wilco. Wilco, Devo. Devo, Jethro. Tull, Tool. Tool, Moe. Moe, Hole. Hole, Korn. Korn, Cracker. Cracker, Limp Bizkit. Limp Bizkit, Hot Tuna. Tuna, Phish. Phish, Byrds. Byrds, Eagles. Eagles, Eagle Eye Cherry. Eagle Eye Cherry, Buckcherry. Buckcherry, Chuck Berry!

Him again? He's just not in sync. More artists are arriving, David Lee, led by my own personal favorite, Sammy Hagar. Hey, do you folks all know each other? No?

Mr. Hagar, Mr. Harding. John Wesley, Leslie. Ms. Gore, Ms. Bush. Kate, Bonnie Raitt. Ms. Raitt, Mr. Strait. George Strait, Tom Waits. Tom, Tim. McGraw, Hill. Faith, Keith. Mr. Richards, Mr. Richard. Little, Baby. Ms. Spice, Mr. Ice. Vanilla, Santana. Santana, Madonna. Ms. Madonna, Mr. Idol. Billy, Billy. Mr. Ocean, Mr. Brooks. Brooks & Gaines, Brooks & Dunn, B&D, Miami Steve. Miami, Houston. Whitney, Britney. Ms. Spears, Mr. Slash. Mr. Slash, Mr. Manson. Marilyn Manson, Zachary Hanson. Zac, Beck. Beck, Boss. Bruce, Juice. Ms. Newton, Mr. Martin. Ricky, Mickey. Mr. Hart, Mr. Beefheart. Captain, Doctor. Dr. Dre, Mr. T. Ice, Ice. Mr. Cube, Mr. Loaf. Meat, Chuck. Chuck Berry! Buckcherry!

Them again? This sounds like a cheap trick, David Lee! Oh well, guess who just arrived! Hey, do you folks all know each other? No?

Trailer Trash

It is a world foretold in man's nightmares.

A world where hope is a memory, and justice, an illusion.*

Where death is truth, and truth is a lie.

And where a lie offers the only hope,

Which, as you may recall, is just a memory.

It is the world of our future.

This summer, prepare for the thrill ride of a life-time.

This summer, prepare to enter the next realm.

On May 31, let the award-winning producer of last summer's most anticipated thriller transport you to a timeless place where dreams come alive, se-cret fantasies run wild, and where the one person you most trust—might just be the one person you most fear.

*Based on a true story.

Because long ago, it was prophesied that this day would come.

The day when one woman dared challenge an empire,

And one man stood at the crossroads between heaven and hell.

And together, they would make the ultimate sacrifice.

And the world would know them by one name . . .

A name that would live forever in the hearts of man . . .

A name to be shouted on the winds of freedom.

And that day is near.

Coming May 31, the people who taught a generation to love and a nation to believe in miracles will unveil a spellbinding tale of magic and wonder, a story as true as the legend that inspired it.

This summer, get ready to laugh.

Get ready to live.

And get ready to fall in love again.

Because inside every heart, there is a secret door.

And sometimes, the key to that door just might be the key to happiness.

And now and then, the one person you thought you couldn't live with—turns out to be the one person you can't live without.

But beware what lurks behind a certain locked door.

Because in this perfect world, something has gone wrong.

This summer, let the award-winning director of last summer's hottest motion picture take you and your family on a different kind of vacation.

No cottage. No campfire. And no turning back.

Be afraid.

Be very afraid.

Be very very very afraid.

Because beginning May 31, evil has a new name.

And only two people stand in its way.

One man.

One woman.

One destiny.

And their names shall be remembered forever,

As long as people believe.

Noel, My Lovely

'**T**was the season to be jolly in Tinseltown, where nine ladies dancing kept eleven lords a-leaping nightly at Club Blitzen, and you didn't need a herd of reindeer to find some very shiny noses. I was on the Ameche, talking turkey to some Scrooges downtown who wanted my neck in a wreath, when the fat man dropped in and helped himself to some milk and cookies I'd left on a plate.

"Next time ring the bell, auld man," I grumbled. "'Cause this ain't your magic toy shop, and I ain't your sugar-plum fairy."

He studied me coldly, two eyes seemingly made out of coal.

"I got helpers who'd deck the halls with you, Sleigh," he spat, raising a bushy white eyebrow roughly the size of Frosty's forearm. "But right now, I got no time to figure out which bulb in your string flickered out. It's crunch time. I believe you got something for me."

I flicked an envelope onto the desk, and he reached for it.

"Not so fast, Kringle," I said. "Before we pass the cranberry sauce, I got a question for you: What's with the babe?"

He snorted three *ho*s, then mistletoed the rest of the milk.

For as long as anybody knew, the fat man ran a huge kiddie extortion racket up north, doling out toys for tots who toed the line, leaving the rest out in the cold. He made boughs of holly, the kind with presidents on it, by using elves as cheap labor. Nobody crossed Claus. You didn't want to end up on his bad list.

Two months back, he'd hired me to keep tabs on Carol, a seven-year-old tyke who lived with her mom in a one-room manger on Cratchet Street. He wanted pictures, tapes, and round-the-clock surveillance, and when I said it'd cost twenty-five dollars a day, plus expenses, the guy's branches never even lost a needle. I figured the kid was a pawn in a custody war, or maybe she'd stayed up late and seen too much. Either way, when the sign on your door says "Nick Sleigh, P.I.," you don't ask questions of any guy who's spreading the cheer.

Besides, bad bets on reindeer games had put me in debt to three wise guys downtown. Unless five hundred dollars appeared under their tree tonight, my Marley would turn up on somebody's door knocker.

For three weeks I tailed the kid. I saw her when she was sleeping. I knew when she was awake. The more I wandered, the more I wondered about the true meaning of my job. It was beginning to look a lot like crassness.

"So tell me," I said. "What's with the babe?"

"Why don't you tell me," he said, lighting his pipe. "Is she naughty or nice?"

Maybe it was the way he said it. Maybe I've seen one too many stockings stuffed with coal. Or maybe it was just the fat man's suit. But I saw red. I reached over the desk, grabbed his beard and yanked him so close I could see the broken vessels where Jack Daniel's had been nipping at his nose.

"Listen, Kringle!" I barked. "I don't care how many chimneys you do on a night! Keep your partridge out of that pear tree, or I'll bust your giblets from here to grandmother's house!"

"O-o-o," he growled, pulling away. "You better watch out."

His eyes drifted to my report. For the next few minutes, he sat back and turned the pages. All was calm.

"Well," he said, when finished. "She's certainly no angel. Forgets chores. Won't go to bed. Cries, shouts, pouts. Looks naughty to me."

"She's a nice kid," I said.

"Yeah, and I'm the Easter Bunny! Listen, Sleigh, this chick sat right on my lap, swore she'd be good for goodness sake, put in for a Barbie Play Set. And look at her room, look! Swaddling clothes. Stockings hung from a chimney—whew, that's gotta stink. Should all offenses just be forgot? Bah!"

"She's just a crazy, mixed-up kid," I said.

"She's bad eggnog, Sleigh. This nymphet, she's been playing you like a string of silver bells. Read your own Yule log! You, yourself, said she doesn't believe."

"Well, why should she? Kringle, you're just like her old man. You show up once a year, make merry, and then it's, 'Up on the rooftop, click-click-click.' "

"I don't write the songs, Sleigh. I just enforce them."

"Go tell it on the mountain."

He gave a strange smile, eyes all aglow, then

flicked a package onto the desk. "Feliz Navidad, chump," he grumbled.

Then he was gone. Outside, bells were jingling, and it had begun to snow. I unwrapped the package, counted up five golden rings. It was just enough to get the grinches off my back. But they didn't matter anymore. The fat man had made his list. And I had made mine. I glanced at the clock. The toy store closed in twenty minutes. To make it, then get to Cratchet Street, I'd have to fly.

ACKNOWLEDGMENTS

The authors would like to thank the following people for their inspiration, assistance, expertise, and/or cold beer: Tom Peyer, Erin Duggan, David McCormick, Dan Menaker, Jeanne Tift, Toby Harshaw, Chip McGrath, Jeff Z. Klein, Ratso Sloman, Chris Knutsen, the former Susan Kelly, Bill Glavin, Jim Johnston, Sharon Green, James Gorman, the Scooter, the Boss, the guy who invented cable TV, and all the people at that extended family of ink-bleeding fools that makes up the Syracuse Newspapers. We owe you big.

Frank Cammuso draws editorial cartoons for the *Post-Standard* newspaper in Syracuse, N.Y. His work has appeared in *Newsweek, USA Today, The New York Times, The New Yorker, The Village Voice,* and *The Washington Post.*

Hart Seely is an award-winning reporter for the *Post-Standard* newspaper in Syracuse, N.Y., whose work has appeared in *National Lampoon, The Village Voice, The New Republic, The New York Times, The New Yorker,* and *Spy* magazine. He is married and has three children.

Throughout 1992, Seely and Cammuso collaborated on a monthly feature called "The Answering Machine," which aired on National Public Radio's *Sunday Morning.*